Oral
Sex

bad
taste
and
hard
to swallow?

Also by Vernon Coleman

The Medicine Men (1975)
Paper Doctors (1976)
Everything You Want to Know
  About Ageing (1976)
Stress Control (1978)
The Home Pharmacy (1980)
Aspirin or Ambulance (1980)
Face Values (1981)
Guilt (1982)
The Good Medicine Guide (1982)
Stress and Your Stomach (1983)
Bodypower (1983)
Thomas Winsden's Cricketing
  Almanack (1983)
A Guide to Child Health (1984)
An A to Z of Women's Problems
  (1984)
Bodysense (1984)
Taking Care of Your Skin (1984)
Diary of a Cricket Lover (1984)
Life Without Tranquillisers (1985)
High Blood Pressure (1985)
Diabetes (1985)
Arthritis (1985)
Eczema and Dermatitis (1985)
The Story of Medicine (1985)
Natural Pain Control (1986)
Mindpower (1986)
Addicts and Addictions (1986)
Dr Vernon Coleman's Guide to
  Alternative Medicine (1988)
Stress Management Techniques
  (1988)
Overcoming Stress (1988)
Know Yourself (1988)
The Health Scandal (1988)
The 20 Minute Health Check (1989)
Sex for Everyone (1989)
Mind Over Body (1989)
Eat Green Lose Weight (1990)
Toxic Stress (1991)
Why Animal Experiments Must
  Stop (1991)
The Drugs Myth (1992)
Arthritis (1993)
Backache (1993)

Stress and Relaxation (1993)
Complete Guide to Good Sex (1993)
Why Doctors Do More Harm Than
  Good (1993)
Betrayal of Trust (1994)
Know Your Drugs (1994)
Food for Thought (1994)
The Traditional Home Doctor
  (1994)
I Hope Your Penis Shrivels Up
  (1994)
People Watching (1995)
Relief from IBS (1995)

Novels
The Village Cricket Tour (1990)
The Bilbury Chronicles (1992)
Bilbury Grange (1993)
Mrs Caldicot's Cabbage War (1993)
The Man Who Inherited a Golf
  Course (1993)
The Bilbury Revels (1994)
Deadline (1994)
Bilbury Pie (1995)

Writing as Edward Vernon
Practice Makes Perfect (novel, 1977)
Practise What You Preach (novel,
  1978)
Getting into Practice (novel, 1979)
Aphrodisiacs—An Owner's Manual
  (1983)
The Complete Guide to Life (1984)

As Marc Charbonnier
Tunnel (novel, 1980)

With Dr Alan C. Turin
No More Headaches (1981)

With Alice
Alice's Diary (1989)
Alice's Adventures (1992)

Oral Sex

bad
taste
and
hard
to swallow?

Vernon Coleman

BLUE
BOOKS

NOTE

This book contains questions and answers which appeared
in the author's column in *The People* newspaper in 1994.

First published in 1995 by Blue Books, PO Box 30,
Barnstaple, Devon, EX32 9YU, England

ISBN   0 899726 02 0

A catalogue record for this book is available from the
British Library

Printed and bound in England by Biddles Ltd., Guildford
and King's Lynn

QUOTES FROM THIS BOOK

'The streets and suburbs are populated by individuals who started out their lives full of hope, ambition and pride but who have, through parenthood, been turned into dull and weary 'grown ups'; suffocated by awesome responsibility and spiritually dead from the hair downwards.'

'I am convinced that the concept of pantyhose was invented by the same secret government department which gave us parking meters, carbon monoxide, and the plastic blow up doll.'

'When your children finally metamorphose into young adults you can get your own back by encouraging them to marry *and to have children of their own!* What joy this thought will bring you. The thought of your grotesque and loathsome offspring, who have taken over your life, cursed with children of their own should bring a smile to your lips on the darkest of days.'

'Stockings and suspenders are an essential ingredient in any civilised society and I am happy to do everything I can to promote their use.'

'Most parents lose any vestiges of hope when their ungrateful children finally turn into whining teenagers. At this point life seems hopeless.'

•Males are fascinated with breasts from birth. For the first six months of life the interest is inspired by hunger. Interest then wanes for ten or twelve years. When it returns it is inspired by lust.'

•If a secretary in London tells you that her boss is tied up she probably means it.'

•You sound an odious, nosy little toe rag and I think you should get back to masturbating in the lavatory with a copy of your wife's underwear catalogue perched on your knees.'

•You have to be a friend to have friends. And true friendships take time to mature. Like seeds growing in the garden you can't hurry friendships; you have to let them take root, you have to be patient and attentive.'

•Strangers will slowly become acquaintances and from those acquaintanceships will be born friendships.'

•The official EU legislation relating to extra marital affairs (strongly supported by all major religions) makes it clear that every hour of illicit sexual pleasure must be subsequently balanced by a week of intense self mortification.'

•Only when it is too late to push the damned things back where they came from do you discover that newborn babies are cute and marginally sufferable only up until the age of about twelve months. After that they gradually become increasingly boring, tiresome and demanding.'

•Since your husband enjoyed a whole night of extra

marital pleasure he owes you eight weeks of hand wringing, a good deal of washing up and at least one new set of shelves in the room of your choice. You are, of course, also entitled to take complete control of the television remote control device for the next two months.'

'Guilt is part of the price that has to be paid when unregulated groin contact sports are enjoyed. Dumping that guilt onto someone else—particularly your partner—is about as sensible as holding a full chamber pot next to the kitchen extractor fan.'

'As many as nine out of ten prescriptions for anti-biotics are unnecessary and it sounds as if your GP is doing her or his bit to keep the drug companies happy by pointlessly prescribing drugs that are more likely to do harm than good.'

'Judging by my mail bag transvestism is consider-ably more popular than hunting, rail travel or the current government and has far more aficionados than country music, bell ringing or anything shown on terrestrial television.'

'Who, I wonder, are the god fearing decent folk whose sensibilities are so tender that they must be protected from exposure to men who prefer pink, silky panties and camisoles to grey Y fronts and string vests?'

'I shall continue to pour scorn on people like you who think that their artificial and paper thin veneer of ecclesiastically based respectability entitles them to look down their noses at everyone else. I'd rather sort sewage bare handed than shake hands with someone like you.'

'All newly weds are encouraged to believe that they are obliged to 'start a family' as soon as they can. This, it is widely understood, is the price that has to be paid for having access to unlimited sexual opportunities.'

'Some people find oral sex in poor taste; others just think it's hard to swallow. But why don't you show your girlfriend what magic you can weave with your tongue? If you take her to places she's never been before she may then be more inclined to recriprocate.'

'You should firmly dissuade your husband from continuing with his newly formed one man Neighbourhood Watch scheme. If a man strips off and is seen getting undressed in his own bedroom by a woman then he can be arrested for exhibitionism, lewd behaviour or, depending on his personal endowment, possession of lethal weapon 1, 2 or 3. On the other hand if a woman strips off in her bedroom and a man who doesn't have an official invitation sees her doing it, he can be arrested as a peeping tom.'

'If one of the unwilling starlets in your husband's private milky way catches a glimpse of him flashing his telescope at her then the secondhand food could really hit the whirling blades.'

'You certainly shouldn't see a psychiatrist if you are at all worried about your mental health. You need to be in tip top mental condition to survive an encounter with anyone in that particular branch of the medical profession.'

‘I don't think you're dotty. If you can still write a sharp letter, spot the plot holes in the average made for TV movie and think of coherent reasons for not voting Conservative at the next election then you're playing the game with a better stacked bag of marbles than most politicians.'

‘If it makes you feel any better I too frequently do daft things. Last Wednesday I went out to lunch. I drove 70 miles with my handbrake full on and when I got there found that I should have turned up on Thursday. I frequently catch trains and then forget why and I have twice fallen asleep during the advertising breaks on TV chat shows. I once went to Bristol when I should have gone to Coventry and if I ever wear matching socks it is nothing to do with me.'

‘Cherish your youthful fantasies and enjoy them to the full. In a few years' time all your waking hours will be spent worrying about mortgage rates, blocked drains and german measles.'

‘Words are merely collections of letters, brought together to express emotions and facts. I believe that it is often easier, and more expressive, to use the sort of short words that most people use and understand than to use long words.'

‘Your girlfriend, who has lived with her breasts for longer than you have, and has probably had to put up with years of sexist abuse, may have grown tired of wise and witty comments like: ‘Cor, look at them melons!' and ‘Wot d'ya feed them on, luv?'

‘I find your cold prejudices, fired by that inspiration

which can be so cruel—a mother's love—as appealing as used incontinence pads.'

'Physiologically, the whole idea of sex is to start a pregnancy. Post orgasmic activity is likely to interfere with this. Nodding off is God's way of ensuring that the sperm that have been fired into position don't get knocked off course by too much leaping about.'

'Your doctor sounds as though he has the brains of a hubcap and as much talent for empathising as mud.'

'You will get a much better idea of whether or not your marriage is going to be a success by standing side by side and cleaning your teeth over the same bowl than you will from clambering into bed and performing sexual gymnastics. If you can put up with the way he squeezes the toothpaste tube from the middle, forgets to rinse the sink and splatters the bathroom mirror with little white flecks, then you are probably made for each other.'

'I wonder why it is that otherwise sane and sensible individuals will always do whatever their doctor tells them to do—even though they would never dream of doing it for anyone else. A friend of mine who is a GP once sent a very respectable and rather pompous bank manager out of his consulting room to collect a specimen bottle from the receptionist's desk. The bank manager did as he was told—even though this meant walking through a crowded waiting room twice. It was only when he arrived back in the surgery, clutching the specimen bottle and looking very red, that my chum realised that he'd sent the bank manager off on this simple errand while he was wearing only his underpants.'

•Completely unreliable research recently established that 57% of accountants' wives spend at least one afternoon a week watching pump and thrust movies.'

•It is, of course, much easier to remain obsessed with the minutiae of life than it is to allow yourself to worry about the big problems. It's far less wearying to look at the trees and let someone else worry about the wood.'

•But it is because millions only ever concern themselves with the trivia—the best way to make a padded pelmet and three ways to eradicate moss from your lawn—that our world has become the obscenely barbaric place it is.'

•Those who concentrate exclusively on keeping their little bits of the planet looking neat and tidy cannot disclaim responsibility for the horrors of the outside world for it is their apathy which has handed over control to the uncaring, the greedy and the inept.'

•Next time your psychologist boyfriend tells you that a squiggle means that you don't love him, ask him why he feels so inadequate and whether or not he has any idea of the cause of his own lack of self confidence.'

•In most people's lives the good luck and the bad luck cancel one another out—and the trick is to try and take the greatest possible advantage of all the good luck so that you can ride all the bad luck.'

•An Indian tribe in Montana was trained to operate a carpet factory. The factory had been built as part of some American government policy of encouraging the

Indians to become more self reliant. The factory ran successfully for six weeks and then the Indians stopped work. When investigators were sent to find out why the Indians had stopped work they were told that each member of the tribe had put a new carpet down in his home and so there was no longer any need for a carpet factory. The empty factory still stands; an enduring monument to an unsophisticated form of logic and an almost childishly innocent approach to life.'

'Isn't life a bitch? Just when you think you've got things sorted out along strolls fate, sneering at all your plans, sending good sense flying out of the window and forcing you to answer questions to which there are never going to be any answers.'

'You have described what is, I suspect, a pretty classical female dilemma: should you stick with the solid, reliable, loving puppy who can put up shelves and mend your car and who will always remember your birthday or should you take your chances with the irresistible charmer who has replaced his fly zip with quick release Velcro and has a little black book that makes the London telephone directory look like a skimpy paperback?'

'You'll regret shacking up with Mr Super Groin when he slopes off with your best pal and leaves you with three kids, two whippets and a five month rent arrears.'

'Some people do get more than their fair share of good luck. Inevitably, that means that others get more than their fair share of bad luck. One guy I know has won the football pools twice. A woman I know has had three different types of cancer.'

'I prescribe cold showers three times a day. Next time you see this girl and feel a stirring in your groin try to believe that you've got a pressure sensitive anti-personnel mine strapped into your underpants.'

'You aren't playing with dynamite. People play with dynamite and live. You are blindfold, naked and drunk and you are juggling with half a dozen petrol driven chain saws while walking a cheese wire above a 5,000 foot drop into a shark infested lake.'

'Of course, you'll have fun. Wonderful gravity resistant breasts. Eager, adoring eyes. Firm skin like soft velvet. But little miss sixteen will wreck your marriage, ruin your reputation and suck you dry.'

'The crisis you are going through will resolve itself in around six years. If things get really bad, clench your fists, stamp your feet, shout, threaten to leave home and tell your teenage daughter that all your friends have much nicer children.'

'You are by no means the only woman who has found that one into two can make three happier. Maybe God meant his advice to be taken seriously when he told us to love our neighbours.'

'It is no coincidence that so many people whose parents were real bastards end up marrying real bastards. They do so because their self respect and self confidence has been shattered and they are, as a consequence, vulnerable, frail and easily manipulated.'

'With Mr Reliable's slippers by your bed you'll always have a fridge that works, your bathroom will be festooned with shelves and he'll always take his boots off before he comes in from the garden—but don't expect too much nude, moonlight sex on Cannes beach. If you go with Mr Nasty then you'll probably regret the decision as soon as you find hard evidence that he's been teaching all your friends the ins and outs of horizontal aerobics and generally banging away like an unfastened shed door in a storm.'

'If I made a list of the world's worst one million sins masturbation would be in the last few thousand, along with picking your nose in public.'

'Aeroplanes carry first aid kits and I'm absolutely confident that stewards and stewardesses love the excitement and challenge of caring for an elderly, sick passenger in mid air. Besides, there's nearly always at least one doctor on board (usually flying off on a tax deductible golfing or skiing holiday masquerading as a training course) and people who fall ill in mid-air have a wonderful fuss made of them. Flying is only really dangerous when the damned planes fall out of the sky and then it doesn't matter how old you are.'

'Any new love affair is exciting. But when you're sexually inexperienced (I assume that you're sexually inexperienced) and struggling to cope with the torment of a pubertal emotional maelstrom, and a fully grown woman with proper breasts and an adult complement of pubic hair tells you that she wants to go to bed with you, the excitement levels must go off any measurable scale. I can quite understand the fact that you can't bear to end this blossoming relationship and your hesitation and apprehension is, in truth, a commendable tribute to your maturity.'

•EU Standard Human Body Equality Regulation FR847/c states that: 'employees of a male gender are entitled to select one week in four when errors of commission or omission, and events of physical clumsiness, must be excused on the grounds of quasi hormonal imbalance'. The regulation goes on to state that male employees must select their weeks of 'substitute menstrual incompetence or incapacity' within seven days of commencing their period of employment.'

•Since sperm have a limited shelf life masturbation gets rid of the old ones and makes space available for new, young, vibrant sperm. Because of this, masturbation can make a man more fertile!'

•Your husband has to accept that you don't want to be handed around the Close like a cookery recipe but you have to accept that he obviously wants his cocoa spiced up with a bit more oomph.'

•Sadly, some women wrongly believe that a husband who dresses in female clothing must be gay. This is nonsense, of course. Gays like men so why would they want to dress up as women?'

•What you should have said, of course, was: "It isn't my penis that is small, doctor. It's your mouth that is big." '

•Your doctor is an early candidate for a gold medal in the 1994 Biggest Plonker Outside Politics Award. If this bloody woman had gone into the diplomatic service we would probably now be at war with the Isle of Wight and busily filling in the Channel Tunnel in an attempt to stop irate foreigners pouring into the country waving big sticks at us all.'

'Someone firm should loosen her corset, pull down her knickers and give her a damned good spanking.'

'I suggest that you take some small comfort from the knowledge that a woman this insensitive will almost certainly be congenitally anorgasmic.'

'As you will, I hope, have already discovered penis size is of no significant consequence to anyone except ballet dancers and women who have had twenty or more children.'

'Sex was originally intended as nothing more than a way of multiplying the species. God wanted us to be able to get on with reproducing ourselves while he got on with his next project. Men have to have orgasms in order to get their sperm into the right position for fertilisation but women's orgasms are entirely super-fluous and serve no practical purpose whatsoever. Consequently, when God invented women he didn't bother too carefully when putting in the orgasm programme. Fear not. Manually stimulated sexual relief has been popular for centuries. It was, indeed, from this source that the phrase 'digital sound' was derived.'

'A recent survey showed that more than half of the population enjoy oral sex so it is, incidentally, the people who are *not* doing it who are abnormal and a bit kinky. Don't let someone else's unfortunate experience affect your own enjoyment of a sex act that gives you both pleasure. Stop listening to other people, keep your head down and enjoy yourself.'

•Most women will put up with shelfless bathrooms, blocked gutters and uncut lawns if they are living with a man who can scramble eggs and whip cream with his tongue.'

•Point out to your daughter that as an attractive and growing woman she is now in possession of dangerous weapons which could cause a great deal of damage if not handled carefully.'

•Being pear shaped is actually relatively healthy. People whose waists are bigger than their hips (apple shaped) are much more at risk of health problems such as heart disease, breast cancer, diabetes and stroke than people with your shape.'

•Porn stars are about as genuine as politicians claiming to be honest, caring and committed. When they fall off the bed, and roll around the room three times, the whole thing is more carefully choreographed than professional wrestling. When he nuzzles her ear and batters his groin against her for the 536th time he is whispering: "Two more minutes of this then when I stiffen and close my eyes you howl like a dog and claw my back. We'll give them long enough for a couple of close ups and then we'll pop down to the canteen for a couple of cheese scones and a nice cup of tea before we film the next one." '

•The average ejaculate contains around 5ml of

semen. If your husband ejaculates six times on each occasion when you make love and you make love five times a day then he would, if he produced an average 5ml on each occasion, produce a litre of semen a week. If all that semen stayed where he'd left it then by the end of just one year you would have ten gallons of semen in your body.'

•Caring is an essential part of curing and nurses who show warmth, compassion, interest and friendly concern in their patients do far more good than all the administrators in the world.'

•When I worked in a hospital casualty department I once saw a female patient who had a buzzing inside her. When I eventually succeeded in catching hold of, and removing, a small vibrator (complete with long lasting batteries) she attempted to deal with her embarrassment by expressing surprise and insisting that she had never seen the device before. When I had washed the vibrator I offered it to her but she refused it, saying that it wasn't hers. She was staying in a nearby hotel and she claimed that the vibrator, which she said must have been left in her bed by a previous visitor, had probably snuck inside her while she was asleep. I am proud of the fact that I showed no obvious signs of disbelief when she told me this.'

•Many marriage experts would be out of business if doctors were given permission to prescribe black stockings, lacy suspender belts, silky camisole tops, peek a boo bras and entirely impractical panties.'

•If he is a transvestite then there is no need to seek any outside help. Many transvestites are better balanced (psychologically) than non transvestites.'

'I think that anyone who tries to convince you that carrying over 100 pounds of unwanted fat is normal, healthy and natural must have the sort of intellectual fire power normally associated with lichen.'

'Any hospital which puts men and women on the same ward must be run by administrators who think of patients as throughput consumables, inconvenient tumour ridden glands and malfunctioning organs, rather than real live breathing, eating, sleeping, farting, feeling individuals.

'If you know of an injustice but do not complain about it before that injustice affects you, then you have no right to complain when it does affect you.'

'Try to forget and forgive. If you can't do both then try to do one.'

'Dreams and memories are there to protect you from the dull and savage days.'

'You have touched love and that is more than some people achieve in a lifetime.'

'Next time you find yourself worrying about something ask yourself how important the worry will seem in ten years' time. You'll almost certainly realise that the worry will have no significance in ten years' time. Then ask yourself how important the worry will be in a year's time or a month's time. You should soon be able to differentiate between real worries—which are likely to have an impact on your life—and superficial worries which have no real importance.'

'A friend of mine who is a gynaecologist swears he can identify all his patients by looking at what he calls the 'business end'. Another friend, who works with him as a nurse, confirms that he will often hurry into a clinic, glance at a patient lying flat on her back with her legs in the air, and then address her by name without so much as a glance at her face.'

'The shape and style of your underwear is unlikely to have any positive or negative impact on your penis's growth prospects. Short term growth is in your girlfriend's hands. Long term growth is in your genes.'

'Why not fuck your way to fitness? Sex is an excellent and under-estimated way to get into shape. Careful selection of positions should enable you to exercise just about every muscle in your body with the possible exception of those responsible for eyebrow movement; though come to think of it, if you surprise one another enough you could even give the eyebrows a workout.'

'It is possible to get fat simply by looking at food.'

'You will have to get used to the fact that after being used as a living, breathing dildo you have been discarded like an old condom.'

'You should try to spend your life doing things that *you* feel proud about. Personal respect is far more important than being able to afford new shag pile carpets and velvet wallpaper every 12 months.'

'Your boyfriend is suffering from a common medical disorder called Niceroundbumsintighttrousersgive-meahardonitis. Other similar diseases include Big-breastsinskintightsweatersmakemyeyespopoutitis and Lovelylonglegsinveryshortskirtsmakemedrivein-tolampostsitis. No treatment is needed, which is just as well since none is available.'

'People can be more stupid, more feckless, more vain, more selfish and more frightened than you could possibly imagine.'

''Neutral', 'objective', 'fair' and 'responsible' are qualities which we are taught to admire. But, in truth, these are the qualities of the weak spirited and the passionless. Name me one great man who was ever 'fair'? Name me a social, technical or artistic advance produced by a 'bland' man.'

'On 12th July 1789 an angry revolutionary called Camille Desmoulins jumped up onto a café table in Paris and made an impromptu, stirring speech which led, two days later, to the storming of the Bastille and the start of the French Revolution.'

'You are simply an insensitive and intellectually deprived thug suited only to a career in politics or the pharmaceutical industry. I trust that your bank balance will always be small, that you will be for ever besieged by worries, uncertainties and guilt and that you marry an ambitious, pushy, razor tongued, ball busting, shopaholic feminist with halitosis, herpes and a moustache.'

'All decent and truly caring parents keep their

children at home, wrapped up in cotton wool, bringing them out for display purposes only when close relatives arrive for tea.'

•If my car inexplicably goes out of control and I end up squashed under a large lorry I hope someone will investigate the accident carefully.'

•You can get rid of about 150 calories by masturbating to orgasm. If you masturbate to orgasm twenty three times that will get rid of a pound of fat. I suggest you produce a book and video about this new diet. You could call it *Toss Off Those Unwanted Pounds* or *Smile Your Way To Slenderness.*'

• "No man and no church shall be judged by the size of their organs," wrote Mrs Confucius, wife of the famous Chinese philosopher and bon vivant, and she certainly knew of what she spoke.'

•Most men suffer from impotence occasionally. I am reliably informed that it happens to male porn stars so often that blue movie directors have stunt organs on hand in case the intended star of the show doesn't stand up to close scrutiny at the most important moment. I suggest you see your doctor.'

•Irascibility and irritability are as much a part of old age as wrinkles, liver spots and thinning hair. Years of frustration and world weariness are probably the primary cause, though physical infirmities and a sad realisation that life really is a bitch are probably contributory factors. There is no treatment for the age related irritability.'

'Elderly relatives who enjoy poor health are like nymphomaniacs in short, tight skirts. Both are difficult to satisfy and impossible to get into and out of motor cars.'

'Time is the most important, most fundamental currency in the world; the only currency that really matters. Unless you are one of the lucky few who really enjoy what you do —and would do it even if you didn't get paid for it—then when you go to work you sell your time for money. And you must then use that money to pay for the quality time in your life. Try to relate the amount you need to earn to what you want to do with your income and try to balance the time you spend earning it against the time that remains for pleasure.'

'If you lived in some other countries (or had been born in a different century) you would be able to go out dressed in a skirt without anyone raising an eyebrow. But I fear that you will be asking for trouble if you try it today. In our guilt laden society there is a real danger that you will be sneered at by the repressed, laughed at by the prejudiced, beaten up by the ignorant and then arrested for causing a breach of the peace.'

'If, as I suspect, you have one of those bolt on heads that can be easily detached then I suggest that you order one of your serfs to remove the whole area north of your neck, place it in a cauldron and boil it for several hours over a log fire. After this treatment your head can be replaced and rebolted and you may find that you are able to think a little more clearly.'

'One of the great ironies (and in turn one of the great injustices) of life is that I get the feeling from my mailbag that those who are responsible for the worst cruelties and injustices with which our world is tainted rarely seem to suffer guilt or anguish as a result of their actions. It is, it seems to me, the innocent and sensitive, frustrated by their inability to stop these outrages, who are tortured by the knowledge of those deeds and who seem to do all the suffering on behalf of the perpetrators.'

'Females suffering from 'tact deprivation' carry folding umbrellas and huge, sensible, imitation plastic shopping bags crammed with spare jumpers, thermos flasks and knitting patterns. Males wear sandals and a haunted look and spend most of their time making sure that they aren't more than 100 yards from a public lavatory. 'Tact deprived' old people often live on coaches and eat in restaurants which triple cook all food so that it is suitable for the artificially dentured.'

'You are roughly 4 stones overweight. Each pound of unwanted fat is a result of an unnecessary 3,500 calories. So that means that you've consumed 196,000 calories that your body didn't need. That's the approximate equivalent of 600 doughnuts too many. Your obesity is not just making it difficult for you to wear a bikini without looking like a 3D map of the butter mountain but it is also hazarding your health.'

'I am reliably informed by those who know that all women in groups talk incessantly and almost exclusively about sex. Your girlfriend and her chums will be talking (and laughing) about the size, colour and shape of your penis, how often you do it, what sexual fetishes you have, how long you can last and so on.'

'Most people get more boring and critical as they get older. When a kid sees a pile of leaves on the pavement he will run through them. Twenty years later that same kid will carefully walk around the pile of leaves. And thirty years afterwards the grown old version of that same kid will complain about the weather, write a letter of complaint to the local council about the danger of wet leaves on the pavements and recommend that all trees be chopped down and be replaced with better public lighting.'

'Even though they may never have seen you naked your girlfriend's pals could probably identify your penis in the dark. They could probably all draw accurate maps of the veins which stand out when you're excited. And I'll give you long odds that they know all about that time you got drunk and tried on your girlfriend's stockings and suspender belt.'

'The battalions of evil are ranged far and wide, high and ugly. They stand firm against the weak and the poor. The meek won't inherit the earth because they have been disenfranchised. But live your life honestly and with good intentions and you will enjoy the comfort of a clear conscience; now probably the only quality asset in a harsh, cruel world.'

'One of the odd truths about our society is that a few people become extremely rich without ever really working while most people work hard all their lives and never make any real money.'

'I bet you a laddered stocking to a St Laurent original

that you've been invited to make a blue movie and you're more likely to be playing Jane the Big Boobed Randy Typist than Ophelia, the fey heroine.'

'Faults are just as much an essential part of any individual character as are virtues. Your boyfriend might be a more admirable character if he was more guarded, less quick to take offence and less likely to act spontaneously. But the zest, the 'punch', the vitality, the piquancy and the talent you admire are a result of a combination of vices and virtues. Remove the vices and you would be left with a very different human being.'

'Those who are silent in the face of wrong doing are as guilty as those who do wrong.'

'Your husband is thoughtless, selfish, unprincipled and contemptible. Leave him. Pack up your belongings and abandon him. He is an evil cad, a foul breathed bounder, an unforgiveable blackguard with no redeeming features and a miscreant with the grace of silage. Your life will be brighter, your future rosier and your world more joyful if you wipe the memory of this dark hearted slubberdegullion from your spirit for ever.'

'I suspect that you may be a Friday person— produced by God when he was looking forward to the weekend. The chances are that a scan will reveal that you have got your brain in upside down and need urgent remedial surgery. Meanwhile, I have arranged for the hospital where you work to keep you on permanent bed pan duty.'

'Around the world the kids who are top in everything at school invariably end up spending their lives as administrators in sewage.'

'People who take jobs as traffic wardens are, like car park attendants, the sort of people who would have worked as gas chamber attendants during the second world war. Your claim that you are 'just doing your job' is the sort of pathetic, spineless whinge that was heard from regiments of war criminals in the late 1940s. The truth is that you have chosen to perform an entirely unproductive and largely pointless task simply for the money you are paid. No one becomes a traffic warden out of any sense of vocation. You are an overpaid, hired thug and have absolutely no right to complain if you are treated with contempt by everyone you meet. I do hope that makes you feel worse.'

'Getting old and never knowing what might have been is almost certainly worse than getting old and having regrets.'

'I know one man who thought that 'putting his affairs in order' meant writing down a list of all the women he'd had sex with and then putting the women on the list in order of preference.'

'Confront your fears and face the worst; it is the unknown which creates the monsters which will engulf you.'

'Owning too much 'stuff' can be bad for you, as there is a real chance that you will eventually be owned by your possessions. There are thousands of people around who don't enjoy life because they are constantly worrying about something happening to their car, their collection of porcelain or their wall to wall snow white shag pile carpeting.'

•You don't have to buy a place of your own in order to have somewhere you can call home. 'Home' is a concept based more on mental attitudes than on the legal ownership of bricks and mortar.'

•This man is a slimy bastard with the soul of a lawyer and the morals of a politician. He could crawl under a carpet without wrinkling it. If you give in to him now there is no knowing where or when his demands will end.'

•There are two sorts of people in this world: the players and the spectators. The players do things, take chances and put their careers, lives and wealth on the line. The spectators criticise and offer their opinions but prefer to stand on the sidelines because they are frightened to take risks.'

•It's a myth that old people are all patient, sensitive and well mannered. Stand in any queue anywhere and you're as likely to get your shins bruised by orthopaedic shoes and carelessly brandished Zimmer frames as you are by Doc Martens.'

•What logic is there in a legal system which results in the arrests of men and women who try to disrupt the hunting of perfectly innocent wild animals while allowing politicians to walk around our streets unhindered?'

•If God had intended us to fly he would have made

aeroplane seats big enough to sit in.'

'A team of highly trained specialists whom I invited to comment on your problem suggested that you take all the usual precautions and bonk yourself senseless. They weren't specialists in human relations, they were car mechanics, but their advice merits serious thought.'

'Nuns have a pretty good life. Other people do all their worrying for them. They don't have to concern themselves with dreary everyday problems and they get to travel everywhere first class.'

'Being a doctor used to mean being part of a profession. No more. Doctors are now just another arm of drug company marketing departments. Clearly, doctors would not need to be bought free meals in order to be persuaded to prescribe important, life saving new drugs. Doctors are given free meals by drug companies trying to flog drugs which may have little or no advantage over existing products. The smaller the advantage the drug offers, the harder the drug company has to try in order to get doctors to prescribe it. You may feel that this means that really crappy drugs are promoted with tremendous enthusiasm and very expensive meals.'

'It makes my heart warm to know that I have reached out and touched so many objectionable bastards in one go.'

'To those who have threatened revenge on the streets I would like to point out that I drive a very old, very large blue Bentley which is far too heavy to tow away and which has wheels which are too large to clamp. You can recognise my Bentley easily because in the place where the Queen's car flies a royal standard my car flies a skull and crossbones. Most traffic wardens are so stupid that when they see the flag they salute rather than give me a ticket and I have every confidence that despite this revelation this state of affairs will persist.'

•What on earth are you asking me for? Your wife's friend is keen to play trains and tunnels with you. Your wife is quite happy about this planned adventure. And instead of getting down to business and making a lonely woman very happy you're wasting time writing to me? My guess is that you must be a civil servant working in some sort of planning department. You have spent so much of your life avoiding responsibility that you are now incapable of making any decisions at all. Actually, I don't think there is much hope for you. Any man who can describe the prospect of fully authorised adultery as 'very nice' has about as much style and soul as a knitted toilet roll holder. Just for the record I seem to remember that D.H. Lawrence, the expert on mining and body part nomenclature, once argued that a natural sexual relationship should involve three, not two, individuals.'

•People who don't get enough sex become irritable, wheezy, mentally stodgy and defaced with wrinkles and liver spots. It was people who don't get enough sex who voted Conservative at the last election.'

•On the whole doctors now do more harm than good. The medical establishment has been bought by the drug industry and today's men and women in white coats are an insult to the memory of Hippocrates and Paracelsus and are little more than a twice paid marketing arm of the international pharmaceutical industry.'

'Take care of your friends. They are the most valuable asset you have.'

'Your loyalty to true friends should take precedence over everything else in your life.'

'True friendship is an asset which will never tarnish and never devalue. And no one will ever be able to take it away from you.'

FOREWORD

I was, so I'm told, the first 'agony uncle' on national television. And several centuries ago I wrote an agony
column for a now defunct magazine for teenage girls. My
columns now appear in magazines and newspapers
around the world. My mail comes in sacks and in
languages I don't even recognise let alone understand. I
receive between 5,000 and 10,000 letters and phone calls
every week. I hate bureaucrats and administrators. I
loathe grey men in suits. I despise politicians, lawyers
and people who tell me what I can or cannot do. I am
probably the only person in the world who has managed
to annoy (and unite) the pin stripes of the orthodox
medical establishment *and* the corduroy jackets of the
alternative medicine establishment. Injustice and cruelty
make me incandescent. I have never had a proper job of
any kind. I am constantly in trouble, constantly being
threatened and for ever being warned that unless I learn
to compromise I will never have a successful career. I do
not own a single item of clothing that could reasonably be
described as 'respectable'. I cannot cook, iron shirts,
unblock drains, put up shelves or maintain motor cars. I
am always losing things. I hate travelling and although
I earn my living as a writer I hardly ever visit the offices
of either the publishers or newspapers I work for. I have
never met most of the people who pay me for the stuff I
write. I cannot understand or operate properly any of the
sophisticated electronic equipment upon which I am
dependent. I am soft hearted to a fault, sentimental and
incurably romantic. I am scruffy and extremely prickly. I
am naive enough and innocent enough to have retained
all my teenage dreams. I am sceptical about the promises
made by the men (and women) in suits and white coats
and cynical about the influence of big business on all our

lives. I hate compromise and am ruthlessly unforgiving. I worry too much...

Why, in the name of everything which is plump and pink, do so many people write to me for advice?

Vernon Coleman
Devon, 1995

ACKNOWLEDGEMENTS

Some readers might imagine that the production of the column wherein the questions and answers which make up this book first appeared would be a solitary occupation. They would be quite wrong. I would like to thank the following for their enormously valuable help and assistance during the last twelve months: Joanne, Sally, Maureen, Fifi, Adele, Nicole, Jennifer, Primrose, Helena, Rita, Sophia, Karen, Grace, Brigitte, Letitia, Daphne R, Daphne L, Mo, Meg, Liza, Kristabel, June, Elaine, Cathryn, Penelope, Hortense, Ruth, Tara, Angela, Beth, Diana, Enid, Stephanie, Zahlia, May, Lesley, Jacquie, Iris, Ophelia, Tara, Imogen, Anna and Ursula.

WARNING

This book is not intended as an alternative to personal, professional medical advice. The reader should consult a physician in all matters relating to health, and particularly in respect of any symptoms which may require diagnosis or medical attention. While the advice and information are believed to be accurate at the time of going to press, neither the author nor the publisher can accept any legal responsibility or liability for any errors or omissions that may be made. Remember: sex can cause pregnancy and spread diseases. Take precautions.

VERY IMPORTANT NOTE

All the letters reproduced in this book have been changed to protect the confidentiality of the individuals concerned. All details have been altered beyond recognition and anyone who thinks they can identify an individual in one of these letters is wrong.

Oral Sex

bad

taste

and

hard

to swallow?

MY WIFE'S PANTIES

I recently found a pair of my wife's panties in my underwear drawer by mistake. I don't know why I did it but I tried them on. I found the sensation so exciting that I kept them on all day and put them into the laundry basket in the evening. Two days later I tried on one of my wife's skirts and put on a pair of her tights and a blouse. I found the experience sexually exciting but also strangely relaxing. I now try on her clothes quite regularly—though she doesn't know, of course. If I know she isn't going to be back home for a while I wear them for as long as I can. I suppose I could stop this strange compunction if I wanted to—but I don't want to. I am 42 years old and happily married. I have always been heterosexual. I run my own successful business and am something of a workaholic. Do you think I could be cracking up or turning gay?

You're not turning gay and you're not cracking up. Men who get pleasure from dressing in women's clothing usually do so for three reasons.

First, the stuff feels nice. Traditionally, men's clothes are made from harsh, unfriendly fibres. Underpants made from Harris Tweed are harder wearing but women's clothes tend to be softer, silkier and far more erotic to the touch.

Second, there's often some deeply hidden, long forgotten and otherwise irrelevant sexual experience behind the desire to dress up in women's clothes. Maybe you got a thrill from touching your mother's silken slip when you were five. Who knows? Who cares? If you've got £20,000 to waste you can probably find a psychoanalyst who'll help you tip toe through your childhood in search of relevant experiences. You can buy an awful lot of pretty underwear for £20,000.

And, finally, you probably feel relaxed when you're dressed in your wife's clothes because the soft, feminine side of your personality is being allowed to surface.

Aggressive, workaholic macho men who put themselves under a lot of pressure do sometimes find that they can relax most effectively when dressed in something soft and slinky. Wearing a pair of silk panties and a silken slip will do you far less harm than knocking back a bottle of scotch or swallowing a fistful of tranquillisers.

I suggest that you pluck up the courage to talk to your wife as soon as you can. Many women often find it surprisingly easy to come to terms with the fact that they are married to a transvestite. Trying to keep your secret from your wife is likely to make things more difficult for both of you—you will have a guilty secret to hide, and when she does find out your wife will have a shock. It might help to point out to her that women often wear men's clothes without anyone batting an eyelid.

··

DISCRIMINATION

I run a small business and employ half a dozen people. I recently tried to fire a black woman who has been consistently late and absent from work and whose unwilling attitude has simply increased the workload of those who work with her. The woman told me that if I fire her she will complain that she is being discriminated against because of her sex and colour.

Threats like the one you have encountered are becoming more and more common. A man who repeatedly failed a simple exam complained that he had been discriminated against because he is 'learning impaired'. (Remember the phrase next time you're looking for the words to describe someone whose intellectual skills do not impress you. It's so much more twee than describing a moron at the council offices as being 'as thick as pigshit'. There is the added advantage that the person you are describing will probably not know what you are talking about. You could, for example, probably describe your political representative as suffering from 'learning impairment' and receive a polite thank you from him in return.) If you are satisfied that neither you nor anyone else has discriminated against this woman and that her work is unsatisfactory, then fire her. If you give in to her, your position will become increasingly intolerable. If you feel that she is trying to blackmail you, warn her that you intend to complain to the police. I believe that blackmail is still a more serious offence than discrimination.

TOO OLD FOR LOVE

I am divorced and have been going out with a man who is much older than me and whom I love very much. He loves me too and treats me like a person—and *that* I never had in my marriage. My problem is that I have a grown up family and although the youngest girl is all for us getting together my son is dead against it. He says that if I marry this man then as far as he is concerned he won't have a mother any more. He says I'm too old to fall in love. You can imagine how this makes me feel.

Have one more try to make your son understand that you and this man love each other. Explain to him that no one is ever too old to fall in love but that everyone is susceptible to loneliness. Make it clear that marrying another man will not affect your love for him at all and tell him how much you need his love, support and friendship.

If he won't change his attitude, then gently tell him that you suspect that there must have been a mistake at the maternity hospital when the babies were handed out and that someone else must have your real son because you could not have possibly given birth to such a mean spirited and prejudiced oaf. You will not be losing a son but a nasty little bigot and you will be better off without him.

BETRAYED

I had been married for five years when I had an affair with my husband's best friend. I slept with him twice. When my husband found out he started divorce proceedings. I only had the affair because my husband had started beating me up quite badly. My husband now tells me that he has been bisexual for the last ten years and that he was hurt by the fact that his best friend had chosen to sleep with me and not him. My husband blames me entirely for the divorce but I feel I have the right to feel betrayed since my husband did not tell me that he was bisexual.

There doesn't seem a lot of point in wasting mental and emotional energy in trying to work out who betrayed whom. You were both at fault—as is usually the case when a relationship breaks down. But I think you should just count yourself lucky that you have escaped from your marriage—not because your husband is bisexual but because if he has been beating you up he is unlikely to stop.

Incidentally, it might be wise for you to visit a sexually transmitted diseases clinic for a check up. If your husband has been actively bisexual during your marriage then he could have brought home more than a wage packet.

....

TOO SMALL

My husband has found out that I have had an affair and he wants to know why. I can't tell him the truth—it would kill him. It's all because of sex, not love. The problem is that my husband is very small. His penis only five and a half inches long and quite thin and I can't feel it most of the time. I try to compensate by making love in different positions but I still never reach a climax. I love my husband but I have had affairs with a number of men—all far larger than him. I must admit that my husband has tried, and still does, but he just isn't big enough. I try not to be unfaithful but I always end up taking a lover for those few extra inches. How do I tell my husband that he is a failure in bed?

What would you think if you read a letter on this page from a man complaining that he had to have affairs with large breasted women because his wife's breasts were too small? You would, I suspect, regard him as a rather selfish, shallow individual and consider the explanation for his wandering rather feeble.

Or what would you say if I told you that I get letters from men complaining that they have had affairs because their wives (after giving birth to two or three of their children) had vaginas which were too large? Might you possibly consider such men to be self centered and inconsiderate bastards?

(Incidentally, since your husband's five and a half inches is perfectly adequate and well within 'average' limits he might well be justified in claiming that it is your physical abnormality—not his—which deprives you of an orgasm during sex.)

The fact is that most women don't have orgasms during intercourse—they need oral or manual assistance before, during or afterwards in order to venture temporarily into heaven. Does it really matter exactly how you get your orgasm? If you really loved your husband then it wouldn't matter a damn. Your determination to obtain sexual satisfaction the way you want it is juvenile and inconsiderate and I'm afraid I find your pathetic attempt to blame your husband for your present mess indefensible.

Maybe he will divorce you and throw you out without a penny. You can then earn your living searching for the perfect penis. I am sure that we would all be happy to know that you had settled down with a big prick.

....

RESENTFUL

When I first got married I really looked forward to having children. But I now have two children (one aged 12 and the other aged 14) and although I love them dearly I'm afraid that there are times when I get fed up and resentful about the way they run my life. Sometimes it seems that every waking hour of my life is spent either looking after them or making money to buy them 'essential' clothes, trips or computer software. They never seem to be grateful for anything that is done for them and they sometimes treat my wife and I as though we are servants.

This is a column about human problems and so I don't usually try to provide advice for or about teenagers, social workers, broadsheet journalists, refugees from the planet Zog, Conservative politicians or others who cannot, by any stretch of the imagination, be regarded as members of the same race as the rest of us. However, the anguish shone out from your letter and so I feel inspired to offer a few thoughts which might be of help.

First, you should be aware that your feelings are by no means unique. The streets and suburbs are populated by individuals who started out their lives full of hope, ambition and pride but who have, through parenthood, been turned into dull and weary 'grown ups'; suffocated by awesome responsibility and spiritually dead from the hair downwards. Men who once concerned themselves with such essentials as the price of real ale and remembering to keep their wallets stocked with condoms, and whose main weekly responsibility was getting up early enough on a Sunday morning to get to the football pitch before the game started, suddenly start worrying about the price of chocolate covered Puff-Puffs, and spend their weekends fitting safety gates to the top of the stairs. Girls who only ever worried about visible panty lines suddenly become obsessed with finding the safest push chair and the best buy alphabet spaghetti.

You say that you looked forward to having children before you had them and I'm sure you are right. All newly weds are encouraged to believe that they are obliged to 'start a family' as soon as they can. This, it is widely understood, is the price that has to be paid for having access to unlimited sexual opportunities. If you think back you will, I suspect, recall that you were heartily encouraged in this aspiration by your parents and your partner's parents. This is significant and I will return to it in a moment.

Only when it is too late to push the damned things back where they came from do you discover that newborn babies are cute and marginally sufferable only up until the age of about twelve months. After that they gradually become increasingly boring, tiresome and demanding.

Most parents lose any vestiges of hope when their ungrateful children finally turn into whining teenagers. At this point life seems hopeless.

I can, however, offer you a chance for the sweetest revenge. Hold this thought close to you during the coming months and years. It will sustain you in your darkest moments.

When your children finally metamorphose into young adults you can get your own back by encouraging them to marry *and to have children of their own!*

What joy this thought will bring you. The thought of your grotesque and loathsome offspring, who have taken over your life, cursed with children of their own should bring a smile to your lips on the darkest of days.

And now, at last, you will realise why your own parents were so keen for you to start a family.

....

DISGUSTED

Your letter about the transvestite in last week's paper disgusted me. You should not print such filth in a family newspaper.

Careful, sir, your repressions are showing right through your prejudices. The strength of feeling you exhibit suggests that you are unconsciously covering up a very powerful desire to dress up in women's clothing. Might I suggest that if you try on something in black satin with a nice lace border you might feel a little more at peace with yourself?

STOCKINGS AND SUSPENDERS

Why do so many of the models who are used to illustrate your comments wear revealing stockings and suspenders?

Because I am convinced that the concept of pantyhose was invented by the same secret government department which gave us parking meters, carbon monoxide, and the plastic blow-up doll. Stockings and suspenders are an essential ingredient in any civilised society and I am happy to do everything I can to promote their use.

BREASTS

Why are men so interested in women's breasts?

Males are fascinated with breasts from birth. For the first six months of life the interest is inspired by hunger. Interest then wanes for ten or twelve years. When it returns it is inspired by lust.

IN THE GARDEN SHED

I am in my fifties and since my wife does not enjoy the best of health our sex life is nonexistent. To obtain relief I masturbate in the garden shed while looking at pictures of naked ladies. The shed is right at the bottom of my garden. A few months ago I inadvertently left the shed door slightly ajar and looked up to see that the woman who lives next door (who is in her late forties) was standing watching me. Since then every time I have gone into the shed my neighbour has gone into her garden and watched. Recently she has taken to stooping down in such a position that I can see that she is not wearing any panties. I feel a great deal of guilt after each of these sessions but I cannot stop myself.

And why should you stop yourself? You aren't doing anyone any harm. You're just a lonely, harmless rake in a garden shed. Leaving the shed door open could have got you into trouble if the neighbour's gnome had seen your garden tool and called in the social workers. But solitary manual labour is nothing to feel bad about and the fact that you have attracted an obviously appreciative audience is more a tribute to your natural skills than a cause for anguish. Your relationship with the woman next door is not exactly usual but I don't think you should lose any sleep over the fact that you are both now members of the same Neighbourhood Watch scheme.

FLAT ON MY BACK

My boyfriend and I were fooling around recently and ended up with me flat on my back on the bed with him lying on top of me. To stop me wriggling he was using one hand to hold my hands together above my head. He then kissed me and started to unfasten the buttons down the front of the shirt I was wearing with his free hand. Finding this difficult to do he pulled out his pyjamas from underneath the pillow. He used one leg of the trousers to tie my left hand to the bed head and one arm of his jacket to tie my other hand to the right hand side of the bedhead. When he had finished tying me up he finished unfastening my shirt and pushed my bra up so that he could kiss my breasts. He clearly found it very exciting to have me tied up in this way. I confess that I was excited by it too. He pushed up my skirt, pulled my knickers and tights down to my knees and made love to me quite aggressively. It was all quite spontaneous and afterwards we both agreed that it had been very exciting. I was quite surprised to find that I enjoyed not having any control over what was happening to me.

Is this sort of sex very kinky? I'd like to do it again and my boyfriend has admitted that he would like me to tie him up next time.

Having sex while one of you is tied up is neither unusual nor kinky. It's very common. An entirely unreliable recent survey showed that 72% of the citizens of London do this at least once a week. If a secretary in London tells you that her boss is tied up she probably means it. Both women and men confess that they enjoy it. Remember that bondage is not about hurting and it should only ever be done with the consent of both partners. Make sure that the knots can always be quickly and easily undone (by the person who is tied up if necessary) and don't ever tie anything around anyone's neck. Don't get into bondage after drinking alcohol and always arrange some sort of code so that if the person who is tied up wants to be released she or he can communicate this information in a way that will be understood. Yelling 'Stop it, oh, stop it you beast!' isn't always taken at face value in these circumstances.

BREAST IS BEST

I like sucking my wife's breasts. Although she hasn't been pregnant for several years she still produces milk which I swallow. Will this do me any harm?

This habit is unlikely to harm you unless you do it in public in which case it may, if you are a notable public figure *outside* the Conservative Party, affect your credibility.

LOSING CONTACT

I wear contact lenses and like to go swimming. Twice recently I have lost a lens while diving into the pool. Can you give me any advice on how to avoid this problem? I don't want to have to give up diving.

Shut your eyes when diving or jumping into the water (after making sure that you aren't going to land on anyone). Or wear goggles. Or you can get larger lenses which are less likely to come out.

WHAT DO LESBIANS DO?

We live next door to two women. I am sure they are lesbians. What do lesbians do together?

What a daft question. What do heterosexuals do together?

Watch TV? Eat spaghetti with a side salad? Play Scrabble? Hoover the stairs and plump up the cushions in the living room? Sew on loose buttons, feed the cat, water the plants and listen to music? If they are lesbians (and just because they live together doesn't mean that they are) and are in love with one another, then they probably also do all sorts of exciting sexual things to one another when you're not looking. And if you haven't got the imagination to work out for yourself what they do, I think you should remain ignorant. You sound an odious, nosy little toe rag and I think you should get back to masturbating in the lavatory with a copy of your wife's underwear catalogue perched on your knees.

AS MUCH FUN AS HERPES

My husband is constantly asking me to let him put a variety of objects inside me—bananas, cucumbers, candles and a roll-on deodorant stick have been just a few of the recent things I've had to put up with. If I refuse we have an argument and he sulks. He took topless photos of me and although he promised not to show anyone he had shown them to a friend within two days. He made a video of us making love and, again, took the tape round to show his friend. I would love to leave him but I have nowhere to go.

Sex games have to be fun and both partners have to be willing. Otherwise they aren't games. Your husband is simply using and abusing you and he sounds about as much fun as herpes would be. Get a job, save your money and within six months you should be able to suggest another site where he can bury his fruit, vegetables and roll-on deodorant.

··

BACK PASSAGE

I have been going with my present partner for several years. Our sex life is very good but some time ago while we were having sex she withdrew my penis and put it into her anus. I was rather embarrassed at the time but didn't show it. Since then she has done this on numerous occasions. She seems to enjoy it very much. Is it dangerous?

Anal sex is far more common than you might imagine. Men sometimes find it enjoyable because the entrance is tighter. Some women claim it gives them a more intense orgasm. Unfortunately, anal sex is the best method of sex for transmitting AIDS. Anal sex is, by the way, illegal so I suggest you empty your bedroom of policemen before you try it.

··

LONELY

I am very lonely. Every one else seems to have friends. Why can't I find friends? I really envy characters on TV programmes who always seem to be surrounded by friends. I would love to be a regular at the Cheers bar.It has now got to the point where I hate going out because the sight of so many people enjoying one another's company just makes me feel lonelier than ever.

You have to be a friend to have friends. And true friendships take time to mature. Like seeds growing in the garden you can't hurry friendships; you have to let them take root, you have to be patient and attentive. If you want long term friendships to flourish you have to be prepared to put yourself out and you must accept the bad days as well as the good. To conquer your loneliness go to more places (pubs, clubs, evening classes) where you'll meet people. Strangers will slowly become acquaintances and from those acquaintanceships will be born friendships.

CONFESSION

My husband has a very good job and works away from home quite a lot but I have never worried much about him meeting someone else. He seldom goes back to the same place and so could never build up a relationship. I have thought about him having a 'fling' but long ago decided that I would rather not know about it. A couple of weeks ago he seemed very quiet and preoccupied. I left him alone for a while but eventually asked him if there was something on his mind. I thought that perhaps he had a problem at work but he confessed that he had slept with a girl he'd met on a flying visit to France. Once he had told me about it he seemed a lot happier. He says he is glad he has told me. When I got upset he couldn't understand why. He said I'd asked him what was wrong and he had told me the truth—and he seemed to think that this made everything OK. I feel very angry—not so much about his one night stand (he assures me that is what it was)—but because he loaded his guilt onto me and now he won't even discuss it. He says it is over and so I should forget all about it. If he hadn't told me I wouldn't have anything to forget.

You are right to be angry. Your husband had the fun and now he's leaving you nursing the hurt and the guilt. And you are quite entitled to expect him to do more grovelling. The official EU legislation relating to extra marital affairs (strongly supported by all major religions) makes it clear that every hour of illicit sexual pleasure must be subsequently balanced by a week of intense self mortification. The legislation is rather weak on exactly what this entails but I gather from advice notes released by Conservative Central Office that you can expect a considerable boost in your housekeeping allowance and, possibly, a small car (between 1 and 1.5 litres, plastic seats and manually operated wing mirrors) as a bonus. Since your husband enjoyed a whole night of extra marital pleasure (a 'night' is officially regarded as 'eight hours' during winter months and 'nine hours' during the summer) he owes you eight weeks of hand wringing, a good deal of washing up and at least one new set of shelves in the room of your choice. You are, of course, also entitled to take complete control of the television remote control device for the next two months.

And make him talk. Tell him that if your relationship is going to survive (and with time it may become stronger than it has ever been) you need to know why he felt the need to find himself in what can perhaps best be described as an 'unofficial legover situation'. Expect to hear words such as 'loneliness', 'availability', and 'boredom' tossed around. And you also want to know what he is going to do about making sure that he doesn't find himself in any more 'unofficial legover situations'.

Finally, let this letter be a warning to any spouse tempted to clear their conscience by 'spilling the beans' about an affair or sexual indiscretion. Guilt is part of the price that has to be paid when unregulated groin contact sports are enjoyed. Dumping that guilt onto someone else—particularly your partner—is about as sensible as holding a full chamber pot next to the kitchen extractor fan.

....

THE ANTIBIOTIC

My eleven year old daughter is a normally healthy child who rarely needs to take time off school. Last Monday she had a cough and so I decided to keep her at home and to telephone the doctor for a bottle of cough medicine. I didn't think my daughter was ill enough to need visiting at home but nor did I think she was well enough to sit in the waiting room with all those sick people. The receptionist told me to collect the prescription later that morning. The medicine the doctor prescribed was an antibiotic. Why did my doctor prescribe an antibiotic for a child with a slight cough—without even seeing her?

Laziness, incompetence, stupidity, a malicious desire to bankrupt the NHS, a dislike of your child—your guess is as good as mine. As many as nine out of ten prescriptions for antibiotics are unnecessary and it sounds as if your GP is doing her or his bit to keep the drug companies happy by pointlessly prescribing drugs that are more likely to do harm than good. The careless prescribing of drugs for patients who haven't been seen is now commonplace and, as a crime of incompetence, exceeded only by the over liberal handing out of repeat prescriptions to patients who don't need them. One elderly reader of this column recently visited her doctor with a cough. After prescribing a bottle of medicine the doctor said: 'Would you like a supply of your usual pills as well?' Puzzled, my reader pointed out that she didn't normally take any pills. Surprised, and apparently not in the slightest bit embarrassed, the doctor confessed that she was the only patient of his over the age of 60 who wasn't regularly collecting 'repeat' prescriptions.

The only advice I can give you is that in future, if a doctor offers you a prescription, always ask whether the drugs are really necessary. A good question to ask is: 'What will happen to me if I don't take this drug?'

....

EXCITING HOBBY

I was very interested to read the letter from the man who likes dressing up in women's clothes. When I first found out that my husband likes doing this I was shocked. For a while I worried that our marriage would be threatened. But I now find my husband's 'hobby' exciting and sexually extremely stimulating. I can still remember the first time I ran my hand up his leg while he was wearing stockings and suspenders. I could, for the first time, understand why men like women to wear them! Can you please tell me how common transvestism is?

No—for the simple but very good reason that most men who like wearing women's clothes are pretty secretive about it. But judging by my mail bag, transvestism is considerably more popular than hunting, rail travel or the current government and has far more aficionados than country music, bell ringing or anything shown on terrestrial television.

···

GOD FEARING FOLK

I was disgusted by your reply to the man who dresses up in his wife's clothes. Anyone who does such a thing is a pervert and should be locked up—well away from god fearing decent folk. Your sympathetic response will merely encourage these people.

Who, I wonder, are the god fearing decent folk whose sensibilities are so tender that they must be protected from exposure to men who prefer pink, silky panties and camisoles to grey Y fronts and string vests? I shall continue to provide sympathetic advice and support to individuals whose harmless fancies and delights attract hatred and venom from people like your bad self. And I shall continue to pour scorn on people like you who think that their artificial and paper thin veneer of ecclesiastically based respectability entitles them to look down their noses at everyone else. I'd rather sort sewage bare handed than shake hands with someone like you.

···

HARD TO SWALLOW?

I want my girlfriend to perform oral sex on me. She says it's dirty. What do you think?

Some people find oral sex in poor taste; others just think it's hard to swallow. But why don't you show your girlfriend what magic you can weave with your tongue? If you take her to places she's never been before she may then be more inclined to reciprocate. You should always make sure that your partner is enthusiastic before trying anything new.

FLUORIDE

I have heard that there are plans to ensure that our local drinking water will soon contain fluoride. Do you think that adding fluoride to the water is a safe practice?

I suggest you campaign strongly against the irresponsible lunatics who want to add fluoride to your drinking water. Fluoride isn't the only potentially dangerous chemical that politicians and scientists want to add to drinking water. It has also been suggested that tranquillisers and contraceptives be put into water supplies—the first to keep people calm and stop them making inconvenient protests and the second to stop them having too many children. If you care about your health (and your children's health) I suggest that you fight the fluoridation proposal very hard. If you bombard local politicians and media with letters of protest then there is a good chance that the plans to poison your drinking water will be abandoned.

BURNED UP BY JEALOUSY

My ex wife has got a new boyfriend and he really pisses me off. I see him when I go over to my ex wife's house to pick up my son on a Saturday. He is good looking, young, drives a smart, new sports car and dresses in really flashy clothes. He makes lots of money and never stops boasting about it. Last weekend I took my son out and my wife's boyfriend insisted on coming with us. He spent a fortune on sweets, ice cream and arcade games—far more than I could afford to spend. And, to cap it all, when we went to the local park he turned out to be a much better footballer than I am. We went down to the lake and he even turned out to better at skimming stones. I feel I am being burned up by jealousy and I don't know what to do.

Children aren't stupid and although they like presents and ice creams and arcade games they tend to know what's going on. Just be yourself. Talk to your son. Listen to him. Have fun with him. Laugh and lighten up. And just remember that you're not in competition with your wife's new beau. There is room in your son's life for both of you. But you're carrying a very powerful trump card: you're Dad and the other guy isn't and never will be. That's probably why he, poor sod, is trying so hard.

....

PEEPING TOM

My husband was given a telescope for Christmas. He has set it up in our bedroom and although he claims that he is using it to look at the stars I think he spends most of his time watching the women across the road getting undressed at night. We live opposite a small block of flats and you can see into quite a few rooms from our bedroom. One woman in particular seems a special favourite. I've seen her myself without a telescope. She is divorced and aged about 45. She has a rather voluptuous figure. She always gets undressed with the curtains open and the light on and I don't think she would complain. I suspect she knows exactly what is going on. But she's not the only one and although I don't think my husband means any harm I'm worried that he could get into serious trouble.

You should firmly dissuade your husband from continuing with his newly formed one man Neighbourhood Watch scheme.

The law is rather sexist about this sort of thing. If a man strips off and is seen getting undressed in his own bedroom by a woman then he can be arrested for exhibitionism, lewd behaviour or, depending on his personal endowment, possession of lethal weapon 1, 2 or 3.

On the other hand if a woman strips off in her bedroom and a man who doesn't have an official invitation sees her doing it, he can be arrested as a peeping tom.

If one of the unwilling starlets in your husband's private milky way catches a glimpse of him flashing his telescope at her then the secondhand food could really hit the whirling blades. And even though you suspect that voluptuous neighbour is an enthusiastic participant in your husband's Neighbourhood Watch scheme, there is a real danger that she may turn him in and recommend him for a porridge diet and a job repairing mailbags.

All things considered I think you'd both be better off if you took the telescope back to the shop and got them to swap it for a train set.

CRACKING UP

I think I am losing my sanity. I do the most stupid things— like putting empty saucepans into the fridge, putting milk and sugar into the teapot and talking gibberish to myself. My mates think I am a nut case. It is very worrying. Do you think I am cracking up? Should I see a psychiatrist?

You certainly shouldn't see a psychiatrist if you are at all worried about your mental health. You need to be in tip top mental condition to survive an encounter with anyone in that particular branch of the medical profession. Newly qualified doctors are only allowed to specialise in psychiatry if they fail a series of simple psychological tests and can show that they have serious mental problems of their own.

I don't think you're dotty. If you can still write a sharp letter, spot the plot holes in the average made-for-TV movie and think of coherent reasons for not voting Conservative at the next election then you're playing the game with a better stacked bag of marbles than most politicians.

If it makes you feel any better I too frequently do daft things. Last Wednesday I went out to lunch. I drove 70 miles with my handbrake full on and when I got there found that I should have turned up on Thursday. I frequently catch trains and then forget why and I have twice fallen asleep during the advertising breaks on TV chat shows. I once went to Bristol when I should have gone to Coventry and if I ever wear matching socks it is nothing to do with me.

....

SEX MAD

I am 18 years old and I think about sex all the time. Am I abnormal?

No. Cherish your youthful fantasies and enjoy them to the full. In a few years' time all your waking hours will be spent worrying about mortgage rates, blocked drains and german measles.

....

PISSED OFF

I object strongly to the language you sometimes use when replying to your correspondents. It is not the sort of language one expects to hear a doctor using.

Sanctimonious and over sensitive souls seem to be increasing in numbers. How do you all manage to breed without getting naked and sweaty? Maybe you simply divide up—rather like amoebae.

I rang up a large company the other day and got told off by a bloke I spoke to for commenting to him that I was pissed off with the service they had provided. Sitting on a horse so high that he would have needed a parachute to dismount he told me that he felt that the words 'pissed off' were offensive.

Words are merely collections of letters, brought together to express emotions and facts. I believe that it is often easier, and more expressive, to use the sort of short words that most people use and understand than to use long words.But I can manage the long words if you prefer them. So, for example, I could describe you as supratentorially deprived and cryptorchid. But would you understand what I meant? And will the insult work if you have to spend half an hour in the library finding out what I've said?

ZINC DISPENSER

Is it true that human sperm is rich in zinc? I keep massaging it into my skin and it helps to keep my complexion clear and young looking. The stuff is cheap, comes in a handy pump dispenser and most partners are happy to assist with its application.

Human semen does contain zinc but no one seems to have done any research into whether or not massaging the stuff into the skin improves the complexion. This is clearly an area where research is vital. I have written to the Medical Research Council and applied for a grant for this important work. I will let you know what happens.

MORE SEX, PLEASE

After dieting for two months I have lost nearly a stone in weight. I have noticed that as I've lost weight so my desire for sex has increased. I used to make love to my wife no more than once a fortnight. Now we do it two or three times a week. Is there a link?

It is quite usual for men who lose weight to feel sexier. Women who have fat husbands and rotten sex lives might well be able to solve both problems with nothing more complicated than a decent diet.

UNEXPECTED ERECTION

I am 64 years old and don't get many erections. When I visited my (lady) doctor recently she insisted on performing an intimate examination. I ended up with a large erection and a very red face. What should I do if this happens again?

Have a willing partner ready nearby and smuggle the erection out of the surgery as quickly as you can. Don't worry about the lady doctor. If she knows what an erection means she'll be flattered.

BIG BREASTS

My girlfriend's breasts are large—she wears a DD size bra. She is very shy about her breasts and always wears clothes that hide them. How can I persuade her to show them off a little more?

What you mean is: 'How can I help you persuade your girlfriend to make you the envy of all your mates?' Women with very large breasts are often shy and embarrassed by their mammary exuberance. Your girlfriend, who has lived with her breasts for longer than you have, and has probably had to put up with years of sexist abuse, may have grown tired of wise and witty comments like: 'Cor, look at them melons!' and 'Wot d'ya feed them on, luv?' Just be grateful that your girlfriend lets you look at and play with her assets and try to respect her feelings a little more.

UGLY GIRLFRIEND

I am very worried about my son. He has just been promoted and everyone says he should go straight to the top. The problem is his girlfriend. She is a nice girl but looking the way she does she could hardly be worse for him. She really is one of the ugliest girls I have ever seen. She has the biggest nose and the smallest eyes you could imagine. To make things worse she has a terrible complexion. When I think of my handsome son lumbering himself with her I could scream. He has had some beautiful girls in the past. Why is he wasting his time with her? I think she may ruin his career if they marry, as the other men will have lovely wives with them at dinners. Apart from that I am worried about what friends and family will think. I get nightmares imagining her face on the wedding photographs. How can I split them up?

I have been sitting staring at your letter for an hour, trying to think of a tactful way to explain to you that there is more to beauty than skin tone and nose size. By the criteria you have expressed you would exclude some of the most attractive and exciting women in the world from your son's attention. (The corollary is that some of the most physically perfect individuals are among the most unpleasant of people and although they might make attractive ornaments they would make hideous partners.)

I find your cold prejudices, fired by that inspiration which can be so cruel—a mother's love—as appealing as used incontinence pads.

But I suppose that what depresses me more than anything is the knowledge that you are right. Your son's career may well be adversely affected if he marries a girl whom you and others regard as ugly. This is not an isolated indictment of the company for which your son works. The bigotry you exhibit is commonplace. I suspect that those who are so corrupted by prejudice that they put appearance above all other qualities are not imaginative or intelligent enough to understand why a happy partnership depends more upon substance than on shape or shadow.

I am, however, somewhat consoled by the thought that if your son loves this woman, and shows more wisdom than his mother and marries her, then disappointment may scar your granite countenance with lines of grief which your hidden rage will constantly fill with tears of frustration and despair. Your own prejudices will, in the end, provide you with the punishment which some would say you richly deserve.

....

SECOND OPINION

I have breast cancer. My doctor has referred me to a surgeon. He says he will take the breast off. Do you think this is really necessary? A friend of mine had breast cancer but the surgeon merely removed the lump.

Please get a second opinion before you allow the surgeon to remove your breast. Occasionally, removal of the entire breast is the best way to treat this type of cancer. But most of the time it isn't necessary and the cancer can be treated with a simpler, smaller operation which only involves removing the cancerous part. Sadly, surgeons don't always bother to keep up to date. There are many vandals masquerading as surgeons who are still hacking off breasts unnecessarily. Any woman told that she needs to have a breast removed should insist on a second opinion. Any decent doctor will be glad to arrange one—and will understand exactly why it's necessary. Never allow yourself to be treated by any doctor who refuses a request for a second opinion. He or she is likely to be suffering from an overly enlarged ego and a lack of self confidence. (Odd as it sounds this is not an unusual combination, by the way. People with falsely inflated egos are often low on self confidence).

TERRIFIED

I think my boyfriend drives far too fast. I hate going out in his car because I am terrified we are going to have a crash. He has had two small accidents already. Whenever I say anything he laughs at me for being frightened.

Tell him that unless he slows down and drives more sensibly you won't get in his car again. And mean it. Don't let him intimidate you by laughing at your fear. In the circumstances you describe fear is a result of intelligence, imagination and experience. Find something your boyfriend is frightened of and you will be able to turn the tables on him. For example, if he is frightened of his mum warn him that you'll tell her if he doesn't slow down. On a skiing holiday I once ended up with an eighteen year old instructor who sneered at me for being afraid when I refused to ski down what looked like a vertical cliff face. The instructor proudly told me that he didn't know what fear was. I like to think that he became a better ski instructor and more rounded human being after I had used a simple, traditional, physical technique to help him to understand the phenomenon. ('Now are you afraid, you slimy little foreigner?' 'Yes, yes, pliss do not my other arm break!') Embrace fear for it is the key to self preservation. Only the quarter witted regard it as a sign of weakness.

OBSESSIONS

I am a happily married woman but from time to time I get obsessions for other women. The women I get these crushes on are usually older than me and invariably rather authoritative, snobby, unattainable types. I don't want a lesbian affair but I do want these women to love me and to want to be with me. At the moment I am completely besotted with a woman I know. The other evening she spent ages talking and laughing with another woman and I was so enraged that I went outside and scratched the side of her car with my keys. Why is this happening to me? What can I do about it?

Freud would have got two textbooks, half a dozen lectures and a monograph out of your confession. I called him up on my ouija board and we both agree that the answer to your problem almost certainly lies in your relationship with your mother. Your desire to be loved by older, slightly distant women suggests that your mother may not have been as loving as you would have liked her to have been when you were small. Recognising this may help you. Even if she is still alive you may not be able to change your mother (if she's dead you'll certainly find changing her an uphill battle) but it may help if you can accept that although she may have failed to show her love, that love was almost certainly there.

....

WHY MEN FALL ASLEEP

Why do most men fall asleep almost immediately after making love? When my first lover did this I thought he was just always tired but I've been to bed with quite a few men now and they are all the same. I don't think it is just a male phenomenon because I confess I often feel sleepy after a good sex session! My problem is that my current boyfriend tends to fall asleep the minute he's come—but I often need several minutes of manual stimulation to reach a climax.

Physiologically, the whole idea of sex is to start a pregnancy. Post orgasmic activity is likely to interfere with this. Nodding off is God's way of ensuring that the sperm that have been fired into position don't get knocked off course by too much leaping about. Men trying hard to make a great impression on a first time lover can sometimes be embarrassed by this phenomenon. More settled lovers may be delighted with the knowledge that sex is an excellent cure for insomnia.

You can solve your problem by getting your boyfriend to take you to orgasm first. Then you won't mind when he falls asleep.

....

HENRY AND I

My doctor and family want me to go into sheltered accommodation. I am 72 years old and quite fit but they're worried that if something happens to me I won't be able to call for help. However, the place they have recommended won't allow me to take Henry, my cat, with me. Henry and I have been together for nine years and I can't bear the thought of us being parted. My doctor even suggested that I should have Henry put down if I couldn't find someone else to look after him.

I suggest that you stand your ground and refuse to move until your doctor or your relatives have found a place where you and Henry can live together. You'll probably need to rely on your relatives since your doctor sounds as though he has the brains of a hubcap and as much talent for empathising as mud.

Despite the existence of an enormous amount of evidence showing that pets are just as important to health as human relationships, some so-called health care professionals still seem to treat cats, dogs and other animals as of no more consequence than cheap furniture. The result of this ignorance can be devastating. Old people who have been made to abandon their pets often become severely depressed and may die of guilt, anguish and a broken heart.

It is not uncommon for elderly or disabled individuals to refuse to move when they are told that they can't take their pets with them. And many old people refuse to go into hospital at all because they fear that while they are away their pets will be removed.

Not all nursing homes and sheltered accommodation cater for pets and that's fine because not all old people want to live surrounded by animals.

But there are places which cater for old people who want to keep their pets with them. And I strongly recommend that you insist on being found space in such a centre.

··

WILL POWER

My girlfriend is overweight and is constantly talking about going on a diet. But she never does anything about it. I know she really does want to slim but I suspect she just lacks the necessary will power. I would like to help her but I'm not sure how to. After all she is the one who has got to do the dieting.

Your girlfriend may, indeed, lack will power. But there are many other possible reasons why she hasn't started dieting yet. Maybe she doesn't know where to find a good diet. She may be afraid of losing weight (more common than you might think). She may just be too shy to join a slimming club. Why not sit down, talk to her and try to find out exactly *why* she hasn't yet turned her words into action? The chances are that she won't know herself until she starts to talk. Once you know what is holding her back, you'll know how you can help her.

In the end, of course, it is perfectly true that your girlfriend's success will depend upon her own determination and will power. You can take your girlfriend to a slimming class but you can't make her slim. But the one thing most slimmers need more than anything else is encouragement and support. Give her that and her chances of success will be boosted enormously.

··

TWO VIRGINS

My boyfriend and I have been together for two years. I am 21 years old and he is 26. He is my first boyfriend and he now wants us to get married. When I told my mother she asked me if I was taking precautions to make sure that I didn't get pregnant. I told her that I didn't need to as my boyfriend and I do not sleep together. My boyfriend wants us both to be virgins for our honeymoon. I thought my mother would be pleased but she was horrified. She said we should sleep together before we get married to make sure that we get on together in bed. I admit I was surprised that my boyfriend hasn't wanted to have sex but I'm not sure what to do now. Do you think I should seduce him to make sure that we are compatible?

Success in bed won't guarantee a lifetime of marital bliss. If it did then I doubt if there would be many divorces these days since most people who get married have already been for a trial run before they sign up. Successful pre-marital nookie is no guarantee that your relationship will last.

If you're going to experiment with sex before you get married (to find out whether or not you are compatible) then there is a whole pile of other things you should try out too. You should make sure that you can put up with the way he eats spaghetti. And you should find out where he cuts his toe nails and what he does with them afterwards. You should spend 24 hours with him the next time he isn't feeling well and you should spend four hours with him stuck in a motorway traffic jam during a boiling hot spring bank holiday. You should help him put up twelve rolls of wallpaper and hand him tools while he puts together a simple, build-it-yourself wardrobe kit.

If you have sex twice a week for the next fifty years you'll have beaten the national average by miles but you will have probably spent no more than 400 to 500 hours getting sticky and sweaty together.

Compare this with the fact that in the same fifty-year period you will have probably both spent around 1200 hours cleaning your teeth.

The conclusion is clear.

You will get a much better idea of whether or not your marriage is going to be a success by standing side by side and cleaning your teeth over the same bowl than you will from clambering into bed and performing sexual gymnastics. If you can put up with the way he squeezes the toothpaste tube from the middle, forgets to rinse the sink and splatters the bathroom mirror with little white flecks then you are probably made for each other.

....

DROP YOUR PANTIES

I am 43 years old, attractive and divorced. I have no husband. I live with my 39-year-old brother. We both caught a bit of flu and went to see our GP. He called us both into his consulting room together and told me to strip first. I stopped when I got down to my bra and panties. 'Come on,' said the doctor, 'Don't be shy. Off with your bra and drop your panties.' My brother had never seen me naked before. I felt awful but did what the doctor asked. All my brother had to do when it was his turn was unfasten the top two buttons of his shirt.

I wonder why it is that otherwise sane and sensible individuals will always do whatever their doctor tells them to do—even though they would never dream of doing it for anyone else. A friend of mine who is a GP once sent a very respectable and rather pompous bank manager out of his consulting room to collect a specimen bottle from the receptionist's desk. The bank manager did as he was told—even though this meant walking through a crowded waiting room twice. It was only when he arrived back in the surgery, clutching the specimen bottle and looking very red, that my chum realised that he'd sent the bank manager off on this simple errand while he was wearing only his underpants.

I could tell you a hundred—perfectly true—stories like that, so I wasn't in the slightest bit surprised to read your letter.

I firmly agree with your unspoken criticism of your GP. In my view it was absolutely wrong of him to have you and your brother in the consulting room together. And I think that it was absolutely wrong of him to get you to undress in front of your brother. The doctor may have been busy but that's only a reason for his behaviour and not an excuse.

I am, however, even more puzzled by the fact that your GP got you to strip off completely. Phrases which I am having difficulty in suppressing include: 'gratuitous nudity' and 'dirty old man'. I cannot think of any appropriate tests which would entitle me as a doctor to require a woman complaining of nothing more serious than a mild attack of flu to remove all her underwear while requiring a man with the same symptoms to do nothing more than reveal a few inches of upper chest.

ILLOGICAL

My uncle smoked 60 cigarettes a day and lived to be 86 years old. My mother has eaten beef all her life and is a very alert 78-year-old. I think this proves that talk about cigarettes and beef being bad for people must be rubbish.

One friend of mine recently survived a serious car accident, another fell out of a building and lived. By your logic this means that neither car accidents nor falling out of buildings are bad for your health.

....

BREASTS TOO BIG

I am 15 years old and quite thin and small except for my breasts. I take a size 38C cup bra. My breasts are much too big for me and there are a lot of things—like sport and dancing—which I do not do because of them. Is there any particular diet or exercise I could follow that would reduce my breast size?

Breasts are largely made up of fatty tissue and a general weight loss programme *might* result in a diminution in the size of your mammary assets. However, there is no way of ensuring that a diet results in a loss of fat from any particular part of your body. If you went on a diet (and since you are not overweight you should not be dieting) you might lose weight from other parts of your body. If this happened then your breasts would look even more out of proportion.

Gaining weight might make your breasts look less exceptional *if* you gained weight everywhere *except* your breasts. But this could go wrong, for if you ate more your breasts could simply get larger while the rest of you remained as slim as ever.

Nor are there any exercises you can do to reduce the size of your breasts. Some chest exercises may help to delay gravity induced droop but they won't turn you into a 38B.

The only guaranteed way of reducing the size of your bosom is to have plastic surgery and I don't think you should even consider this for another five years at least. You may be much taller by then and considerably happier with the size of your breasts. You may have grown to love them and to be grateful for God's bountifulness.

Meanwhile, buy and wear good, supportive bras and you should be able to dance and exercise as much as you want.

ADDICTED TO PORN

I am 18 years old and have never had a boyfriend or any sexual experiences. I feel that I am too ugly. Recently I have taken an interest in pornographic movies. They make me feel very sexy and I can reach a climax while watching them. I watch two or three of them a night and can't relax without them. I come home from work excited and impatient to watch them. Do you think I need professional help?

No. But I do think that you need more self confidence and more contact with other people and you're not going to get either sitting stuck in front of a video recorder watching two professionals pretending to have sex with one another. You need to get out and about a bit more and to establish new routines for yourself. Try calling in at a health club on the way home from work. Enrol in a painting class. Take up hockey, aikido or macrame.

Meanwhile, don't feel bad about the fact that you get turned on by porno movies. Research has shown that women are just as likely to enjoy dirty films as men are—though they're probably less likely to admit it. Completely unreliable research recently established that 57% of accountants' wives spend at least one afternoon a week watching pump and thrust movies.

THE UNCARING, THE GREEDY AND THE INEPT

I work with a group of women who only ever seem to talk about housework. They talk incessantly about the price of groceries and how often they wash their curtains. I like to keep my home reasonably clean and smart but I can't get excited about any of these things—and they certainly don't seem to be a reason for living. Do you think I am odd in this?

No. And before either of us gets accused of sexism I think I ought to point out that men are just as likely as women to become obsessed with the mechanics of living instead of getting to grips with life itself. Walk into your local pub on a Sunday morning and you'll find crowds of men wittering on about their twin stroke, four bore, double ended carburettors and about double hammer, triple action home tools that can drill holes in sheet steel. Down at the golf club men will be chuntering about bank charges and slug control and convincing themselves that they are tackling the world's real problems by engaging in earnest banter about the latest bizarre and fashionable but irrelevant exhibition of neo-native finger painting. In any pub, club or supermarket nappy changing facility the talk is far more likely to be about the goings on in television soapland than the desperate need for a revolution.

It is, of course, much easier to remain obsessed with the minutiae of life than it is to allow yourself to worry about the big problems. It's far less wearying to look at the trees and let someone else worry about the wood.

But it is because millions only ever concern themselves with the trivia—the best way to make a padded pelmet and three ways to eradicate moss from your lawn—that our world has become the obscenely barbaric place it is.

Those who concentrate exclusively on keeping their little bits of the planet looking neat and tidy cannot disclaim responsibility for the horrors of the outside world for it is their apathy which has handed over control to the uncaring, the greedy and the inept.

THE ENTERTAINER

When I got married 3 years ago my husband had a good job. However, he was recently demoted and we have found it hard to manage financially. He has started to blame me—saying that I cannot manage the housekeeping budget. He works with a man whose wife apparently does wonders with their income. I assumed that this other couple were probably in debt but I recently met the wife in a department store. I was waiting to pay for some stockings. She was paying cash for a very expensive suit. We got chatting and went for a coffee. I asked her how she managed so well. At first she just laughed and said she was careful but suddenly said that she would tell me if I promised not to tell my husband—or hers.

I learned that she visits a house in a nearby town two days a week and 'entertains' businessmen. Her husband has no idea but is happy to accept their very comfortable standard of living. She has invited me to join her and says that there is plenty of work for another woman.

I refused but last night my husband had another go at me—saying that I cannot manage his money and referring again to this couple. I couldn't tell him the truth behind his workmate's lifestyle but it all seems very unfair and I am now very tempted to join this other woman. What do you think I should do?

Sit your husband down with a large piece of paper and a pencil and explain to him exactly where every penny goes. Prove to him that you are managing his money as efficiently as anyone possibly could.

He should then realise that his friend's lifestyle must be being sustained by an extra income from somewhere.

If you want to become a prostitute because it's a career you've always found attractive, then that's fine. But don't, for heaven's sake, drift into it so that you can try and con your husband into believing that you can feed five thousand with a handful of fish and a few small loaves.

....

LADDERED STOCKINGS

My husband and I are both in our 30s. He is more highly sexed than I am and to get satisfaction my husband masturbates. I know this because I asked him how he gets relief when I won't have intercourse. I don't mind him doing this as it is better than him straying to another woman. He does it when there is no one in the house. The problem is that I think he wears my stockings and suspenders when he masturbates. Quite a few times my underwear drawer has been rummaged in and when I've gone to put my stockings on they have been stretched or laddered. I must admit that I was worried at first but the more I think of it the more it excites me. Sometimes I myself even masturbate while thinking about him in my nylons. I wish he would wear them when we have sex but do not know how to approach him and raise the subject.

Next time you're making love tell him you read a letter in a newspaper about a woman whose husband wears stockings and suspenders when they make love. Tell him the idea turned you on. And ask him if he'd like to try it. But do make sure that there isn't anything on the floor for him to trip over when he leaps out of bed and dashes for your lingerie drawer. He may well break the world record for the six foot sprint.

Try not to notice if he seems exceptionally nifty when handling a suspender belt.

DOODLE BUG

My boyfriend is a psychology student. Every time I do or say anything he finds a sinister interpretation. While I was talking on the telephone the other day I doodled all over the front of the phone book. When I'd finished, my boyfriend snatched the book off me, spent fifteen minutes studying all the squiggles and then told me that I clearly didn't love him and had a fixation on my father. I am terrified to speak or do anything in case it is misinterpreted.

Turn the tables on him. Next time he tells you that a squiggle means that you don't love him, ask him why he feels so inadequate and whether or not he has any idea of the cause of his own lack of self confidence. When he tells you that a chance remark means that you are secretly longing to run off and open a basket weaving factory in Corfu, ask him why he always dresses like a homosexual.

Next time he tells you that a doodle on your shopping list means that you hate your great grandfather's cousin's next door neighbour's dog, ask him if he is aware that his mannerisms clearly indicate that he has a wild crush on his maternal grandmother.

He will either go potty, shut up or leave.

....

FROM CRISIS TO CRISIS

Everything seems to happen to me—everything that can go wrong does go wrong. Other people seem to sail serenely through life but I just lurch from one crisis to another. Why is this? What am I doing wrong?

You may not be doing anything wrong. Everyone gets luck of both sorts. In most people's lives the good luck and the bad luck cancel one another out—and the trick is to try and take the greatest possible advantage of all the good luck so that you can ride all the bad luck.

But it's true that some people do get more than their fair share of good luck. Inevitably, that means that others get more than their fair share of bad luck. One guy I know has won the football pools twice. A woman I know has had three different types of cancer.

However, it's not all down to luck. There is no doubt that some people do manage, through their behaviour or attitude, to attract trouble. Then, when trouble arrives, they have an unhappy knack of making things worse for themselves.

And some people have a habit of unconsciously building up ordinary everyday problems into crises—partly because their lives are empty and the presence of the crises makes them feel important and significant, partly because the crises are an excuse for failures in other areas of their life, partly because they want sympathy and partly because crises are, by definition, exciting and attention attracting. Some people seem to enjoy lurching from crisis to crisis; the dramas making them feel more alive.

....

LOVE AT FIRST SIGHT?

I am in my early forties. I've been married and I'm fairly sensible, sane and cynical. I live in a tourist area of Italy so, not unnaturally, I meet a lot of holidaymakers. Last year half a dozen guys came over to play golf for a few days. I got chatting to one and we went out for drink. I am fairly cynical about men and have never believed in love at first sight but I really fell for this guy. What's more he seemed to feel the same way. He told me that his wife had died three years earlier. We met every night, made love (which was wonderful) and really seemed to feel at ease with one another. Two nights before he left he told me that he had booked a flight back here in about three weeks' time and was going to stay with me for a couple of weeks to try and persuade me to return to the UK with him. He held my face in his hands, looked directly at me and said: 'I promise I'll never hurt you and I'll never run out on you.' I promised to wait for him and trusted him absolutely.

He never came back. He hasn't written or phoned and I am absolutely heartbroken. I never thought that he was lying to me because there was no reason for him to lie. He gained nothing from it. He wasn't trying to get me into bed because we had already done that. I hadn't asked him to return. I hadn't asked him for anything.

I can understand that people on holiday get carried away and then reality strikes when they get home but surely he could have sent me a note. For 59 minutes of every waking hour it goes round and round in my head. Why did he say all those things if they were lies? Why deliberately hurt me?

Maybe he meant what he said but lost his nerve when he got back to reality; and maybe he now feels guilty about letting you down. Maybe he lied about his wife dying. Maybe he lied about his job or about how wealthy he is and now feels embarrassed. Maybe he is a real heel and simply wanted to create a fantasy future and you were unwittingly playing a part in his fantasy world.

Maybe he is a lying, cheating, psychopathic bastard who gets a kick out of hurting people.

That's a lot of maybes. And a lot of uncertainty.

Even if he didn't give you his address (and if he didn't then you should fear the worst) you should be able to trace him through the hotel or holiday company with which he travelled. If they won't give you his address tell them you've just found some documents he left behind and ask them to forward an envelope to him. Write to him and ask him to get in touch with you. If that doesn't work write again and tell him that unless you get a reply you'll travel to England to see him. If he has something to hide that should produce a reply.

....

THE JOBBING BUILDER

My husband works for himself but is very unambitious. He runs his own small business and whenever he thinks we have enough money in our bank account he just stops work until most of the money has gone. He is a jobbing builder and turns down a lot of work—particularly during the summer months when the weather is good. He just switches on the telephone answering machine and goes fishing. How can I persuade him to take his responsibilities more seriously? I don't want him to become a workaholic but I do the books and last year he had a total of 12 weeks holiday and even during the weeks when he worked he never worked more than a 40 hour week.

Your husband will probably live a healthy, happy life. While towns full of workaholics are digging themselves into early graves he is enjoying himself and guaranteeing himself an extra couple of decades of stress free life.

When I read your letter I was reminded of an Indian tribe in Montana which was trained to operate a carpet factory. The factory had been built as part of some American government policy of encouraging the Indians to become more self reliant.

The factory ran successfully for six weeks and then the Indians stopped work. When investigators were sent to find out why the Indians had stopped work they were told that each member of the tribe had put a new carpet down in his home and so there was no longer any need for a carpet factory. The empty factory still stands; an enduring monument to an unsophisticated form of logic and an almost childishly innocent approach to life.

Your husband will probably never be rich in cash terms. But he will be happy. And you can be too. Don't try to change him. Enjoy the lifestyle he has created for himself.

∙∙∙

ONE BIG PARTY

I went out with one boy for six months and we were really happy together—life with him was like one big party. After I twice saw him with other girls I finished with him. After that I met another boy who I have been going out with for several months. He has been really good to me. He says he loves me and he buys me presents and I like him quite a lot. But now the first boy wants me back. He admits he treated me badly but he says he wants us to get engaged. I don't know whether to trust him after last time. Everything is made more complicated by the fact that the boy I have recently been going out with will be very hurt if I finish with him. I think he'd like to marry me too.

Isn't life a bitch? Just when you think you've got things sorted out along strolls fate, sneering at all your plans, sending good sense flying out of the window and forcing you to answer questions to which there are never going to be any answers.

You have described what is, I suspect, a pretty classical female dilemma: should you stick with the solid, reliable, loving puppy who can put up shelves and mend your car and who will always remember your birthday—or should you take your chances with the irresistible charmer who has replaced his fly zip with quick release Velcro and has a little black book that makes the London telephone directory look like a skimpy paperback?

If you stick with Mr Reliable then the chances are that in a couple of years time you'll start secretly wondering whether life with Mr Nasty might not have been more exciting.

With Mr Reliable's slippers by your bed you'll always have a fridge that works, your bathroom will be festooned with shelves and he'll always take his boots off before he comes in from the garden. But don't expect too much nude, moonlight sex on Cannes beach.

If you go with Mr Nasty then you'll probably regret the decision as soon as you find hard evidence that he's been teaching all your friends the ins and outs of horizontal aerobics and generally banging away like an unfastened shed door in a storm.

The comfortable, reliable one sounds about as much fun as a mustard poultice. You obviously don't love him.

And you'll regret shacking up with Mr Super Groin when he slopes off with your best pal and leaves you with three kids, two whippets and a five-month rent arrears.

Dump them both and wait until you find someone you like *and* love.

....

MISSING UNDERWEAR

I am a female student living in a house with my boyfriend and another male student. Recently I noticed that some of my underwear had gone missing. I thought nothing of it until I went into the other man's room to borrow a textbook and to my horror noticed one of my bras under his bed. I didn't say anything and now I don't know what to do. Should I tell my boyfriend or should I confront the guy and see what he has to say?

I think this is probably the time for subtlety rather than confrontation. Tell the guy you know he took your underwear and ask him why. There are several possible explanations. First, he might have taken your underwear as a masturbatory aid. If he has, then tell him that you'd rather he supported his fantasies with someone else's smalls. Second, he might have taken your underwear because he wanted to wear it. If he admits to this, then suggest that he buys his own. Third, if he confesses that he has fallen in love with you (and you haven't fallen in love with him), then it would probably be wise to suggest that life for all of you will be easier if he moves out and finds somewhere else to live. If he tells you that he borrowed your bra to use as a catapult, because he needed to carry two melons home from the supermarket or so that he could complete a structural engineering project, tell him you'll give him thirty seconds to come up with the truth or else you'll shop him to your boyfriend.

THE WORRIER

My wife and I recently went on our first holiday for three years. As soon as we got there she started talking about all the things she'd got to do when we got back. Over the six years that we've been married I've noticed that she does this a lot. Whatever we're doing she always wants to talk about the thing we're going to do next. We recently decorated the living room together but instead of enjoying the results she now just talks about what she wants to do to the kitchen. Even when we're making love she finds other things to talk about. She's always worrying about stuff that might or might not happen and she's always making lists and plans for the future. How can I persuade her to take more interest in the present?

Tell her what you've noticed. Be tactful and gentle about it but tell her. Ask her to try and slow down a little—for both your sakes. Life is hard enough at ordinary speed. Your wife is running with the turbo booster on and the throttle jammed open. Try and persuade her to smell the flowers she's grown before she worries about the next planting.

....

THREE NIPPLES, TWO BREASTS

My girlfriend has three nipples. The extra one is just under-neath her left breast. She is very self-conscious about it and gets quite embarrassed if I mention it or draw attention to it. How unusual is this?

Lots of people (male and female) have a spare nipple. Try not to make a big thing of it. I'm not surprised she's self-conscious about it if you point it out to people. I have this terrible vision of you standing up on the beach shouting: 'Hey, folks, look at this! My girlfriend has got an extra nipple!'

....

TORRID AFFAIR

My husband recently found out that I had had a brief, casual and rather torrid affair with a man I met through my work. It wasn't a love affair—it was just sex. My husband made me tell him all about it. He wanted to know what we'd done together, how often we'd done it, where we'd done it and so on. He wasn't satisfied until I'd told him everything in great detail. He even made me describe the other man's penis. Afterwards my husband made love to me quite fiercely. It was the best sex we've ever had. He didn't say anything but I got the impression that my confessions had excited him. And I suspect he would like me to do it again with someone else. Could I be right?

You could be. Some men do get excited by the knowledge that their partners have been making love to other men. But I strongly suggest that before you follow your hunch you talk about this. Even if he gets turned on by your infidelity your husband will probably want to lay down some ground rules. Safe sex at all times. Nothing indiscreet. No anal sex. That sort of thing.

TEENAGE CRUSH

I am 42 years and quite happily married. The family next door have a 16-year-old girl who seems to have developed a crush on me. Whenever I see her she flirts with me outrageously. At first I was embarrassed but I confess that I have recently found her attention flattering and exciting. My wife was out of the house yesterday and she came round to ask me to help her with some homework. She was wearing a very short skirt, a thin T shirt and little or nothing else. While we were sitting together on the sofa she got closer and closer to me. She was pretending to take an interest in what I was writing in her notebook but she obviously wanted me to kiss her and in the end I did. I'm absolutely certain that if I had wanted her to go further she would have been quite happy to do anything I wanted her to do. I don't know what the hell to do now. I would dearly love to take her to bed but I have a suspicion that I'm playing with dynamite.

Whoa! Down boy! I prescribe cold showers three times a day. Next time you see this girl and feel a stirring in your groin try to believe that you've got a pressure sensitive anti-personnel mine strapped into your underpants.

You aren't playing with dynamite. People play with dynamite and live. You are blindfold, naked and drunk and you are juggling with half a dozen petrol-driven chain saws while walking a cheese wire above a 5,000 foot drop into a shark infested lake.

Of course, you'll have fun. Wonderful gravity resistant breasts. Eager, adoring eyes. Firm skin like soft velvet. Magic, stolen, secret moments of loving. And then she will fall in love with a spotty 17-year-old and tell her Dad about you. Blame. Wagging fingers. Cruel accusations. Little miss sixteen will wreck your marriage, ruin your reputation and suck you dry.

I suggest that you smile sweetly when you see her but make sure you're never alone with her again.

....

THE ANNOYING BOYFRIEND

My boyfriend really annoys me. He is only ever concerned
with himself. I am very concerned about a wide variety of
political issues. I campaign about cruelty to animals and
about environmental abuses. But he won't get interested in
anything. He says it's all a waste of time. He says that *they*
won't ever take any notice of people like me so I'm wasting
my time writing letters and going on marches. All he is
interested in is his career, his car and having a good time.
He works as a television presenter and when I try to get
him to use his position to help my campaigns he refuses,
saying it would damage his career to get too involved. I'm
beginning to think that we might not be very well suited.

The world is divided into two groups of people: those who
are selfish, narcissistic and self obsessed and those
whose concern for themselves is tempered or even over-
whelmed by their genuine concern for some other aspect of
life.

Individuals in the first group tend to become politicians
or TV presenters and acquire far more power, money and
fame than is good for them or anyone else. They find it difficult to understand why people like you get so upset about
things that don't directly concern them.

People in the second group suffer endless agonies of guilt,
frustration and anger because they know what is wrong
with the world, they want to put it right and yet they find
that those in power won't listen to their screams of outrage.

You, I'm afraid, are one of the unlucky ones. You are in
the second group. You *care*. And you won't ever be able to
escape from that burden.

Say goodbye to your shallow boyfriend. Your relationship
has no future. He won't change and you can't. He will
become increasingly irritated by your seemingly illogical
commitment to change the world and you will find his
conceit, self satisfaction, arrogance and aloofness increasingly insufferable.

. . . .

INHIBITED

My wife and I have been married for nine years and have two lovely children aged six and eight. Unfortunately, we are never likely to add to our family since our sex life has more or less completely dried up. We used to have terrific sex together but these days the children always seem to be around and even at night my wife is constantly worried about them coming in and finding us. On the rare occasions when we do try and do it I find the need to be quiet inhibiting to say the least. Things have got so bad that when we recently left the children with my parents and went away to a hotel it was a total disaster. I couldn't even get an erection. It isn't just our sex life that has suffered. We never seem to have time to do anything together any more. We used to talk and laugh and share things—now everything revolves around the kids.

If you allow things to continue the way they are then your marriage will soon begin to founder. The lack of sex is bad enough but your current failure to find time to communicate is likely to have an even deadlier effect on your relationship. I fear it won't be long before one or both of you starts looking for extracurricular sex and companionship. As the seventeenth-century philosopher Sir Ramick Hobbs once said: 'Neither man nor woman can live for child alone'.

What is happening to you is very common. The pressures and responsibilities of parenthood often mean that all the love and time that is available gets spent on the kids—with the result that there is none left for sharing between partners. Since children have a quite insatiable appetite for both love and time, it's no good waiting for them to say: 'Hey, you two guys should have some quality time together!' Wait for that and you'll wait too long. Don't expect them to give you time together—take it, guard it, treasure it and use it!

You need to teach your children to respect your relationship as man and wife. You should explain to them that you need private time for one another (just as they will want time and space to themselves) and that just as you won't enter their room uninvited so they must respect your privacy.

And, just in case the little bastards are slow in learning, put a lock on your bedroom door—and use it!

....

FIERCE ROWS

I am having terrible rows with my thirteen-year-old daughter. She disagrees with everything I say and some of the rows we have are frighteningly fierce. I have never known anything like it before and it frightens me.

I'm sorry. I only give advice about how to deal with human relationships. Teenagers do not fit into this category. I can only suggest that you hold firm and try to stay calm. The crisis you are going through will resolve itself in around six years. If things get really bad clench your fists, stamp your feet, shout, threaten to leave home and tell her that all your friends have much nicer daughters.

....

SHARED HUSBAND

My husband and I are both in our forties and enjoy each other's company very much, but he has always been much more highly sexed than I am. Recently I found that I just could not keep up with his demands. He was exhausting me. The solution to my problem came as I was talking to a friend who was recently widowed and in her mid fifties but still very smart and attractive. For three years now we have been satisfying my husband's sexual requirements between us. I am very happy with this state of affairs. My husband and I have grown closer together now that we have found a solution to this, our only problem.

Thank you for telling me about your success. I get armfuls of letters every week and many of them are from people whose lives are in a mess so it was a real delight to get a letter from someone who has found a practical and lasting solution to a potentially disruptive problem!

As you have discovered for yourself the best solutions do not always fit in neatly with society's expectations. Some individuals would probably frown disapprovingly on the way in which you have found happiness and mutual satisfaction but I know from my mail bag that the most enduring solutions are often the most surprising and most imaginative.

I know of many other similar relationships up and down the country and you are by no means the only woman who has found that one into two can make three happier. Maybe God meant his advice to be taken seriously when he told us to love our neighbours.

··

SELF ABUSE

As a child I was abused by my father. My wife, who was much older than I am, said only immoral men wanted or enjoyed sex. After our babies were born she would start to sexually arouse me and then turn over laughing. For the last 25 years of our marriage I masturbated. I continued to do so after my wife's death. Recently I was talking to some people I met who are very religious. They listed some sins and said that self abuse was one of the worst things a person could do. They say that God will never forgive me and that I will burn in hell. As a result I am very ashamed of what I did to myself and I do what I can to atone for my sins. I deny myself this sexual release. What is your opinion? Is what I did a truly terrible sin?

It is no coincidence that so many people whose parents were real bastards end up marrying real bastards. They do so because their self respect and self confidence has been shattered and they are, as a consequence, vulnerable, frail and easily manipulated.

Since an overwhelming susceptibility to guilt is a

common result of a lack of self assurance such individuals (and you are clearly in this category) are also commonly abused and taken advantage of by religious groups.

I suspect that the manipulative, spiritually jackbooted maniacs who told you that masturbation is a major sin were either intellectual sadists, the sort of people who get their kicks out of making other people suffer, or else after your money, your obedient support and your soul (probably in that order). I'll lay 10 to 1 in guineas that full atonement will eventually require regular cash donations.

If I made a list of the world's worst one million sins, masturbation would be in the last few thousand, along with picking your nose in public.

You have done nothing to be ashamed of. Masturbation is a perfectly natural, healthy way for a lonely individual— male or female—to find sexual release. Just about every animal in the world masturbates from time to time.

Please have nothing more to do with these cruel people. I will pray to my God, an altogether more compassionate being, that you find a kind and loving partner with whom you can share body, mind and soul but until then—carry on masturbating!

....

GOING TO AMERICA

My mother and I plan to go to America in the summer but I am worried that at her age flying may be dangerous. What do you think?

Buses are dangerous. Lifts are dangerous. Walking across the street is dangerous. Trains are dangerous. Cars are dangerous. Bicycles are dangerous. But sitting in an armchair can be dangerous. And lying in bed too much is very dangerous. If her doctor says she is fit to fly and the airline will take her, then go—though make sure you both buy health insurance for America because doctors and hospitals there are notoriously reluctant to treat anyone who isn't either fully insured or swathed in a thick layer of dollar bills.

And don't worry! Aeroplanes carry first aid kits and I'm absolutely confident that stewards and stewardesses love the excitement and challenge of caring for a sick passenger in mid-air. Besides, there's nearly always at least one doctor on board (usually flying off on a tax deductible golfing or skiing holiday masquerading as a training course) and people who fall ill in mid-air have a wonderful fuss made of them. Go and enjoy. Flying is only really dangerous when the damned planes fall out of the sky and then it doesn't matter how old you are.

....

I KISSED MY TEACHER

I had what I thought was a crush on one of my teachers. Since then I have found out (through eye contact and her touching me) that she feels the same way about me. I now realise that I really do love her. I have kissed her and this week she asked me to make love to her. I know that you would advise me to bring all this to an end but I can't bear to finish it.

I can understand your dilemma. I'm sure that what is happening to you is exciting. Any new love affair is exciting. But when you're sexually inexperienced (I assume that you're sexually inexperienced) and struggling to cope with the torment of a pubertal emotional maelstrom, and a fully grown woman with proper breasts and an adult complement of pubic hair tells you that she wants to go to bed with you the excitement levels must go off any measurable scale. I can quite understand the fact that you can't bear to end this blossoming relationship and your hesitation and apprehension is, in truth, a commendable tribute to your maturity.

One of the reasons why society tends to punish adults severely when they have sex with children (and however well developed you may be, in the eye of the law you are still a child) is because adults are supposed to be better able to deal with temptation.

To say that your teacher is behaving irresponsibly is surely an understatement of monumental proportions. Your teacher is behaving so stupidly that there has to be a chance that she is mentally ill.

If you go to bed with your teacher someone will find out. And when they do, you will share a considerable amount of pain. Your teacher will have done to her career what she would have you do to her. The only good advice I can give you is to somehow find the strength to turn down this opportunity. If you are convinced that your love will last (and I am sure you are) then maybe you could try to persuade your teacher to move to another school so that you can give your relationship a chance to mature.

If, despite all this advice, you find the call of your loins too strong to ignore, just make sure you use a condom.

EQUAL RIGHTS

Why should women expect to be treated equally? I work with a woman who demands equal rights but for one week every month she takes time off and expects to be excused her mistakes because of 'hormonal' problems. If men and women have equal rights why shouldn't I be entitled to one week every month when I can blame everything I do wrong on my periods?

Stop whingeing. The problem you outline has already been dealt with by the bureaucrats. EU Standard Human Body Equality Regulation FR847/c states that: 'employees of a male gender are entitled to select one week in four when errors of commission or omission, and events of physical clumsiness, must be excused on the grounds of quasi hormonal imbalance'. The regulation goes on to state that male employees must select their weeks of 'substitute menstrual incompetence or incapacity' within seven days of commencing their period of employment. This facility is available only to men under the age of fifty—after that Regulation CD2390/f becomes operative.

PROMOTION

My husband recently applied for a promotion at work and in order to oil the wheels a little we invited his boss and his wife around to dinner. I hadn't met my husband's boss before but thought he was very charming and attractive. The next day, after my husband had gone to work, his boss called round to bring me some flowers as a 'thank you'. I made him a coffee and we got chatting. He made it pretty clear that he found me attractive and hinted that if I slept with him he would give my husband the job he wanted. I am afraid I was all too eager. But when we made love it was very disappointing. He had no idea of foreplay and came within 30 seconds of putting his penis inside me. He then rolled over and fell asleep. I was left feeling very frustrated and couldn't wait for him to leave.

My husband got his promotion and I got rid of my guilt by telling myself it was worth it to see him so happy.

But the next week, while my husband was at work, his boss came around again. When I told him I didn't want to go to bed with him again he said that if I refused he would sack my husband. Since then he calls round at least once a week and has sex with me (it isn't making love). I hate every minute of his company. How can I get out of this situation?

Call the bastard's bluff. Point out to him that if he sacks your husband and ruins your life you will take him down with you. Explain that if he carries out his threat you will report his infidelity to his wife. Warn him that you will encourage your husband to sue him for wrongful dismissal—and point out that you will entertain the resulting tribunal and the listening journalists with a blow by blow account of his sexual inadequacies. I very much doubt if you will hear any more from him.

Indeed, I suggest that once you have told him your plans, and just before he leaves with his tiny tail tucked between his legs, you tell him that you feel that your husband deserves a bigger office, a more seemly pension plan and a much more expensive motor car.

RUNNING LOW?

Is it possible to run out of sperm? Masturbating is my favourite hobby and I am worried.

You will not run out of sperm. Indeed, since sperm have a limited shelf life masturbation gets rid of the old ones and makes space available for new, young, vibrant sperm. Because of this masturbation can make a man more fertile! Incidentally, I was impressed the way that you described masturbation as a hobby. I wonder who will be the first celebrity or MP officially to list masturbation among his or her hobbies and interests.

RESPONSIBILITY

A lot of people near where I live have animals but don't look after them properly. I know one house where 20 rabbits are kept in two small cages. And I know people who have dogs but never take them for walks or look after them. People who acquire animals as pets should realise that there is a lot of responsibility involved.

Looking after animals properly takes time and money—and is a long term commitment. If you know someone who doesn't look after an animal properly you have a moral responsibility to report them to the police—once you've done this make sure that the police take action to stop the cruelty. (If they hesitate, point out that mistreating an animal is behaviour likely to cause a breach of the peace).

NO ORGASMS

I have been married for 35 years. In all that time I have never experienced an orgasm. I recently telephoned your Helpline and discovered what I have been missing all these years. However, I can only achieve an orgasm by masturbating and it takes quite a long time—half an hour or more. I cannot achieve an orgasm through penetration and my husband gets tired or bored long before I've reached an orgasm through masturbation. Why does it take so long? A friend in whom I confided told me that it only takes her five minutes to climax.

L ots of women take a long time to journey into never-never land. And it is abnormal for a woman to get there through ordinary, penetrative sex. So there is nothing wrong with you. But since thirty minutes is long enough for cramp and muscle fatigue to affect the most ardent lover why not share the digital duties with your husband? And don't be afraid to enlist some battery aided support.

NEW NEIGHBOURS

Last year we inherited some money and bought a new house on an exclusive housing estate. We were rather worried that our new neighbours would look down on us but they turned out to be very friendly and we soon got invited to parties, dinners and so on. Then at a barbecue we discovered that they were into wife swapping and wanted us to join them. I was quite shocked and horrified when my husband told me that he was keen. I told him that I had no intention of sleeping with any of the men or letting him sleep with any of the women. He insists the neighbours seem happy with what he describes as their 'hobby' and says he can't see why we shouldn't join in.

Since then I have avoided the neighbours but my husband continues to be friendly with them. Every time he goes out into the garden, or works on his car, one of the women appears and starts chatting to him. Now I daren't leave him alone in the house in case something happens. I feel like a prisoner and I am terrified that he is going to get involved. I want to move but he doesn't. Although I don't want to join in the partner swapping I sometimes feel that if I agreed then at least I would know what was happening rather than being tortured by suspicion.

Moving house won't stop you feeling suspicious and—unless you move to somewhere suitably remote and well away from civilisation—won't stop your husband having a little extracurricular nookie. Come to think of it, even if you go somewhere really remote—an igloo in the Arctic Circle, a tent in the Sahara or a semi-detached in Coventry—he won't necessarily stop thinking about it.

You and he need to talk about this. You both have to find out how you can put sparkle and excitement back into your sex life. He has to accept that you don't want to be handed around the Close like a cookery recipe but you have to accept that he obviously wants his cocoa spiced up with a bit more oomph.

There are lots of ways in which you can make things more exciting. For example, I get heaps of letters from women telling me that their love lives have been revitalised by a handful of indecent lingerie. Or maybe you could experiment with a little bit of fantasising or role playing. Dress up in something two sizes too small and get your hubby to take you out for a drink in a hotel bar.

Your neighbours' hobby need not threaten your marriage if you are prepared to acknowledge that your husband's eagerness to get involved suggests that your marriage needs some restoration work.

●●●

FIRST SEX

I had my first sex when I was a boarder at a girls' school. It was with the matron and she was a wonderful lover. Since then I have enjoyed an exciting sex life with girls and women. After school I started an intense affair with a woman I was working with. I found out that she was making love to her son, and with her encouragement I went to bed with them both. I eventually paid the price by getting pregnant. I had the child—a son—who was aware of my female lovers as he grew up. When one particular affair ended I was distraught and my son was a great comfort to me. He then became my second male lover. I still sleep with him though I also enjoy lesbian affairs. I have read in your column about relations between a brother and a sister and wonder how many cases of caring but incestuous relationships there are.

Before I started to write this column I honestly thought that loving, caring, incestuous relationships were as rare as honest Tories. They aren't—they are quite common (loving, incestuous relationships that is—honest Tories are as rare as ever).

The type of incest that seems to work successfully most often is that between mother and son. Oedipus would be applying to himself for a pardon if he knew what was going on in the shires and suburbs of this pleasant land. Countless thousands of incestuous couples enjoy one another despite the constant fear that their forbidden love will be exposed and attacked. Many cases of incest are exploitative, tragic and devastating. But those who are most vocal in their condemnation of incest, and those whose response to the very word is automatic revulsion and criticism, should be aware that there are many for whom this type of relationship is satisfying and fulfilling in every sense.

We should, of course, do everything we can to protect the innocent. But when we protect the innocent we should take care not to harm those who are not guilty; those whose only crime is to follow a lifestyle and a form of loving which falls outside the pattern of what we have been taught to think of as 'normal' behaviour.

SUMMER HOLIDAY

I have been asked by a group of friends to join them on a summer holiday. I am male and single and would love to go. My problem is that I have thick hair on my arms, legs, thighs, stomach and chest and would feel embarrassed about being seen in a swimming costume. I've been hairy for as long as I can remember and I never wear short-sleeved shirts or shorts because of my hairiness—and I never take part in any sports which involve going into changing rooms. I'm not keen on using hair removal cream because I have so much hair and I am worried about the effect it would have on my skin. I have never been abroad and I don't want to miss this opportunity but I don't know what to do. Having so much body hair has made me very depressed and has stopped me developing normal relationships with girls. I feel that I am missing out on everything. When I was 14 my mother took me to my doctor. He wondered if I had a hormonal problem and he arranged for me to see a hospital specialist. They examined me but could find nothing wrong.

Your sort of hairiness is almost certainly something you've inherited. And your background could have an influence. People of Mediterranean descent—Greek, Italian, Jewish or Arabic—are most likely to be exceptionally hairy.

Not all that many generations ago we were all covered in hair—it was there to keep us warm. When the air temperature is cold you can see the vestiges of the system at work: individual hairs will stand on end in order to trap a layer of air next to your skin and keep you warm.

It isn't going to be easy to remove all that unwanted hair. The best and most effective way to remove unwanted individual hairs is electrolysis—in which a tiny electric current is used to kill the hair roots. But removing hair from your whole body would take for ever and cost an arm and a leg.

My advice is that you buy yourself a small pair of good scissors and a pack of disposable razors and shave the stuff off. (Don't wash it all down the plug hole because if you do you'll probably block the drains.) It'll take weeks—maybe months—for the hair to grow back thickly.

I suggest you do this because I can tell from your letter that reassurance isn't going to work. But your fears are unfounded. Most people aren't going to stop what they're doing and stare at you just because you've got hairy legs. A few will—but you may be surprised to hear that some of them will be women who are actually turned on by hairy men.

I THINK MY WIFE WROTE TO YOU

In your column recently you included a letter from a woman who suspected that her husband was dressing up in her underwear when she was out and who was secretly excited by the idea. Everything in the letter suggested that it was my wife who wrote the letter—and if it was then her suspicions are absolutely accurate. I do dress up in her clothes and I do find it terrifically sexually stimulating and I would love my wife to share my pleasure. You advised the woman to tell her husband that she had read about men dressing up in women's clothing and to ask him if he would like to try it but so far my wife has said nothing. How long should I wait? Have you had many letters like the one you printed? Should I tell my wife that I am a secret transvestite?

I get DD cupfuls of letters from men who enjoy dressing up in women's clothing. But all the letters I print (about this or any other topic) are disguised so that the people who wrote them cannot be identified. You must, I'm afraid, make up your own mind about whether or not to tell your wife. Ideally, you should tell her. Secrets burn holes in relationships. But there is a risk that she will be horrified by your confession. I have had very sad letters from men who have told their wives about their peccadillo and then seen their marriages crumble. Sadly, some women wrongly believe that a husband who dresses in female clothing must be gay. This is nonsense, of course. Gays like men so why would they want to dress up as women?

NOT VERY PRIVATE

When I visited my doctor for a very private examination she asked me if I minded if a medical student sat and watched. I said it would be all right. During the examination the doctor, quite unnecessarily I thought, commented on the size of my penis. 'My word, haven't you got a small penis!' she said. She turned to the medical student and pulled a face. I was very upset and embarrassed and I can't stop thinking about what she said.

What you should have said, of course, was: 'It isn't my penis that is small, doctor. It's your mouth that is big.' Your doctor has shot straight into my list of the Ten Most Thoughtless and Stupid Doctors in the World. She is outright winner of this month's 'Foot'n'Mouth Trophy' and an early candidate for a gold medal in the 1994 Biggest Plonker Outside Politics Award. If this bloody woman had gone into the diplomatic service we would probably now be at war with the Isle of Wight and busily filling in the Channel Tunnel in an attempt to stop irate foreigners pouring into the country waving big sticks at us all.

Someone firm should loosen her corset, pull down her knickers and give her a damned good spanking. You could probably make a formal complaint about her but that would simply extend your embarrassment and publicise the whole miserable business. I suggest that you find yourself another doctor—preferably one who isn't as big a bozo as this one— and take some small comfort from the knowledge that a woman this insensitive will almost certainly be congenitally anorgasmic.

As you will, I hope, have already discovered, penis size is of no significant consequence to anyone except ballet dancers and women who have had twenty or more children.

··

PINK DISEASE

My mother tells me that when I was little I nearly died of something called 'Pink Disease' and that she was told at the time that the disease would leave me prone to infections for the rest of my life. No one—not even a young doctor friend—has ever heard of this disease. Can you tell me what it is?

I haven't heard of this since I was a medical student back in the 1840s! I'm not surprised your doctor friend has never heard of it for the disease from which you suffered isn't even mentioned in modern textbooks. 'Pink Disease' describes a type of poisoning which resulted when children were given teething powders containing mercury. Unless the illness left you with any obvious weakness I suggest that you forget about it.

I can't explain why parents used to give their children teething powders containing mercury. But nor can I explain why so many modern parents give their children vitamin and mineral supplements.

....

NO CHILDREN

From the moment we met I made it clear to my husband that I didn't want children—and he agreed. However, he is now going back on this agreement. We argue a lot about this (it is the only thing we argue about) and I have told him my feelings but he thinks we have a duty to have children. When I point out the problems our friends have with their children he insists that ours won't be like that. Part of the problem is that my husband's mother is desperate for grandchildren and she puts a lot of pressure on him. He has recently suggested that we stop using condoms for 12 months and let fate decide. He says that if I don't get pregnant in that time he will stop pressing me for a family. I feel like agreeing—just to stop the nagging—and secretly going on the pill for the 12 months to make sure that I don't get pregnant. Do you think I could trust my doctor to keep this secret?

I am fascinated by the thought of you making it clear right from the outset that you didn't want children. I have this vision of you and your husband being introduced at a party, him making some bland and nervous comment about the weather and then struggling to keep his jaw up when you announce that don't intend to have any children by him.

That's the small talk over. I thought we ought to get into

this gently because I suspect you won't like what I'm going to say.

You can, I hope, rely on your doctor not to spill the beans. But I have to tell you that I am appalled that you should even contemplate deceiving your husband in this cold blooded way. Most marital deceptions are inspired by unplanned, hot blooded lust. Such indiscretions are far more excusable than the scenario you describe.

Are you really prepared to let your husband make love to you for twelve months under such dishonest circumstances? Are you honestly prepared to fake surprise and disappointment each month when it becomes clear that the previous month's semenal offerings have fallen on stony ground? And are you prepared to live with your fraud for the rest of your life? I suspect not. I certainly hope not—for your sake as much as your husband's.

Sadly, your marriage has hit one of the biggest rocks in the sea of life. And there is no easy solution. There is no available compromise. You can't have a bit of a baby or become part-time parents.

You and your husband have to keep on talking. You both need to express your fears and to define the ways in which you think having—or not having—children will affect your lives. There may be ways in which you can conquer or control some of those fears and anxieties. But in the end one of you has to give in—one of you has to be disappointed—or else your marriage is over.

Life ain't easy, is it?

KEEN NUDIST

My girlfriend is a keen nudist and wants me to go with her and her parents to a nudist camp for a week's holiday. I am very nervous about it. I am worried that with all those naked women around I will have a constant erection.

Stop worrying. Most men who have never been to a nudist camp wonder how the male nudists manage to avoid getting thumping great boners all the time but the men who patronise these places always insist that all that unadorned naked flesh simply isn't sexually arousing.

I suspect that you'll find that you soon get used to all the naked bodies around you. And until you do, embarrassment will keep your erectile mechanism under control. (Besides, if you're going to a nudist camp you'll be so bloody cold that people will probably need a magnifying glass even to see your penis—let alone to spot what sort of condition it is in.)

Crude and dimwitted pornographers always produce pictures of completely naked women which are about as arousing as a stumble through a varicose veins clinic but skilled movie makers and photographers have known for years that too much nudity is simply not erotic. The most erotic, exciting and stimulating images are those in which the imagination is given encouragement by glimpses of breast, and a few half hidden and titillating hints of naked thigh.

....

DIGITAL SOUND

I am a 22 year old woman. I can only reach an orgasm when I or my boyfriend touch my clitoris, or the area around it. I don't seem able to have sex through inter-course. Am I odd?

Not in the slightest. You have to remember that sex was originally intended as nothing more than a way of multiplying the species. God wanted us to be able to get on with reproducing ourselves while he got on with his next project.Men have to have orgasms in order to get their sperm into the right position for fertilisation but women's orgasms are entirely superfluous and serve no practical purpose whatsoever. Consequently, when God invented women he didn't bother too carefully when putting in the orgasm programme. Fear not. Manually stimulated sexual relief has been popular for centuries. It was, indeed, from this source that the phrase 'digital sound' was derived.

••

HAPPILY MARRIED

My husband and I have been happily married for ten years and our sex life has always been very good. For years I have loved to give him oral sex, which he enjoys very much. However, when I told a friend about this she made me feel that oral sex is rather sordid and dirty. It just hasn't been the same for me since and I haven't been able to bring myself to do it any more. An important part of our sex life has gone and I am very sad about it.

You didn't really think that you were the only couple practising oral sex, did you? A recent survey showed that more than half of the population enjoy oral sex so it is, incidentally, the people who are *not* doing it who are abnormal and a bit kinky. Don't let someone else's unfortunate experience affect your own enjoyment of a sex act that gives you both pleasure. Stop listening to other people, keep your head down and enjoy yourself.

And, incidentally, I hope he returns the compliment. Most women will put up with shelfless bathrooms, blocked gutters and uncut lawns if they are living with a man who can scramble eggs and whip cream with his tongue.

••

SKIMPY BRA

My husband died when my daughter was a baby and I have brought her up alone. We have always got on very well and although I have had occasional affairs they have always been short lived and never very serious. I recently met a man whom I really liked and a few months ago he moved in with us. I was a bit frightened that my daughter might try to grab more of my attention but instead she is flaunting herself at my boyfriend. She wanders around in a very skimpy bra and knickers, leaves the door wide open when she is having a bath and lies sprawled on the floor or sofa in such a way that he cannot help but see right up her skirt or dressing gown. When I spoke to her about it she said she was just behaving naturally because she felt comfortable with him around but I have seen her flirting with him and she has a very knowing look in her eyes. I know exactly what she is doing. I wouldn't worry if my boyfriend had just laughed it off but he seems fascinated by her.

I am sure that you're absolutely spot on. Your daughter fears that she's lost you and so she's going to grab the man out of your life, teach you a lesson and satisfy her own blossoming yearnings all at the same time. To make things even more explosive your daughter has been deprived of adult male company for most of her life so is probably pretty inexperienced in dealing with men. And now, just as her hormones are all of a flutter, she finds herself in a situation where she can safely flirt and flaunt herself, punish you and investigate her own sexuality. The whole situation is an emotional bloodbath. I'm not suggesting for an instant that your daughter has deliberately sat down and worked all this out. She is, I suspect, simply reacting to a cluster of provocative stimuli: jealousy, anger, fear and unrecognised and unbridled teenage lust. What is happening is so predictable that to be honest I think you would have been justified in feeling alarmed if she hadn't responded in this way. Then you might have had a real problem.

Of course, I realise that none of this helps you deal with the fact that your daughter has sharpened her hook and cast her line and your boyfriend may be about to take the bait. Your daughter is female. Your boyfriend, being male, does not stand a chance of coping. He will be out manipulated every step of the way unless he is constantly on his guard.

Your first move should be to talk to him. Explain to him that your daughter is inexperienced with men, uncertain of her sexuality, immature, vulnerable and probably angry and confused about her relationship with you. Tactfully, ask him to be careful. Tell him you know very well that you can trust him and that he would never dream of taking advantage of your daughter's innocence but point out to him that you're worried about him. Explain that teenage girls with vivid imaginations and too many uncontrolled hormones not infrequently make startling allegations about abuse and molestation. If he has any functioning cerebral matter he will hear alarm bells and will in future be more careful.

Then talk to your daughter. Explain to her that this is a difficult time both for you and your boyfriend as well as for her. Make it very clear to her that your love for her has not changed at all. And point out to her that as an attractive and growing woman she is now in possession of dangerous weapons which could cause a great deal of damage if not handled carefully. You will need to exercise great restraint and show a good deal of tact during the coming months. Take every opportunity to talk to your daughter and to tell her how much you love her.

PEAR SHAPED

I am very pear shaped—my waist is quite slender but I have an enormous bum and very large hips. Nothing I do seems to change this.

Then you are clearly intended to be pear shaped. But take heart! Being pear shaped is actually relatively healthy. People whose waists are bigger than their hips (apple shaped) are much more at risk of health problems such as heart disease, breast cancer, diabetes and stroke than people with your shape.

PORN STARS

How do porn stars make sex last so long? They do it for ages but I can never manage to keep it up for more than five minutes at the most. And how come the man's penis never falls out when they're making love and rolling around on the floor?

Simple: they're only pretending to do it. All that huffing and puffing and screaming and squealing is fake. Porn stars are about as genuine as politicians claiming to be honest, caring and committed. When they fall off the bed and roll around the room three times, the whole thing is more carefully choreographed than professional wrestling. When he nuzzles her ear and batters his groin against her for the 536th time he is whispering: 'Two more minutes of this then when I stiffen and close my eyes you howl like a dog and claw my back. We'll give them long enough for a couple of close ups and then we'll pop down to the canteen for a couple of cheese scones and a nice cup of tea before we film the next one.'

....

TOO MUCH SEX?

When I got married I was pleased when I discovered that my husband was 'highly sexed'. But I am now becoming increasingly worried. We have sex five times every working day—before we get up, before he goes to work, when he comes home for lunch, when he arrives home from work and when we go to bed. At weekends we have it more often. Although he is 33 his ejaculation seems to go on for several minutes. He is so potent that he can climax up to six times in any one love making session. I am worried about the amount of sperm going into my body. Will it have any long term effect if we continue as we are now?

The average ejaculate contains around 5ml of semen. If your husband ejaculates six times on each occasion when you make love and you make love five times a day then he would, if he produced an average 5ml on each occasion, produce a litre of semen a week. If all that semen stayed where he'd left it then by the end of just one year you would have ten gallons of semen in your body and your whole neighbourhood would smell of horse chestnut blossom.

But I don't think you need worry. Prostitutes cope with heavy sexual activity without blowing up like barrage balloons because gravity ensures that most of the semen trickles out in between love making bouts. This process can be aided by showering and bathing regularly. The enthusiasm of the French for coital sports explains the popularity of the bidet in that country.

You may also be able to gain some slight consolation from the thought that your husband's production of semen will be almost certainly be rather less than that of a less sexually active individual.

PENIS FOR SALE

I was interested to read that surgeons find it difficult to provide proper genitals for women wanting to become functional men. If surgeons write to me I will be willing to sell my penis (seven inches long when erect) and testicles for £1,000,000. I have fathered healthy children but am willing to call it a day on the subject of coition for recreation or procreation. I would like to buy a Rolls Royce motor car since our Ford is now over ten years old and is beginning to give us troubles mechanically. I had to have the ignition switch replaced recently and was warned that the cam belt will soon need replacing at a considerable cost. I would also like to have a reliable urine disposal arrangement. If a buyer is found ready and able to meet the terms of my offer I will give you exclusive photos.

NB I have not discussed the above with my wife yet so be prepared to cancel the offer if she objects.

I really do think you ought to speak to your wife before you continue with your plan to start flogging off the family jewels. I have no doubt that a surgeon could transplant your penis and testicles onto a woman keen to acquire male physical characteristics but fear that the price you are asking might prove to be rather a stumbling block—particularly when you remember that fees for surgeons, lawyers and surveyors would have to be added on top of your million. Transsexuals are not particularly common and I would imagine that millionaire transsexuals are about as thin on the ground as thoughtful, sensitive politicians. I can't see many bank managers being eager to offer mortgage facilities to would-be purchasers of your reproductive equipment, in fine condition (one careful owner) though it might be.

THE TALKING NURSE

I have been a patient in hospital for two months. I am recovering from a stroke. I have been constantly kept cheerful by one of the junior nurses. She works hard but she has always found time to smile, say hello and even talk to me for a little while. A few days ago one of the administrators spotted her talking to another patient and gave her a very severe ticking off. Since then she has hurried by without looking at me or anyone else. Do you think it would be worthwhile writing a letter, pointing out how much patients appreciate these little signs of kindness?

Yes, I certainly do! Address your letter to the senior administrator. Caring is an essential part of curing and nurses who show warmth, compassion, interest and friendly concern for their patients do far more good than all the administrators in the world.

NOT AN EASY MAN TO LIVE WITH

I have been married for 26 years. My husband is not an easy man to live with—he is selfish and bad tempered—but I stayed with him for the sake of the family. I thought things would be easier when our children grew up (he was always having rows with them) but in fact things couldn't be much worse than they are now. The only thing my husband lives for is his work. He never had a very high sex drive but he hasn't made love to me for a year and when I try to make the first move he always says he is tired and not interested and would rather have a hot meal. If I try to kiss him and he is smoking he won't even take the cigarette from his mouth, but just gives me his cheek to kiss. I long to be held and made love to but it never happens. I try to talk to him and he tells me he has been talking to customers all day long. He just sits in front of the TV and falls asleep. What can I do? I just feel like walking out. I am stuck in a rut, and bored. I feel so lonely that I might as well be on my own. At least then I wouldn't have to put up with his moods.

I think you should try to build up other aspects of your life before you seriously contemplate leaving your grumpy and unromantic husband. If you do leave home you will need a source of income, somewhere to live and friends if you are to create a new life for yourself. So expand your interests now. If you don't have an outside job think about finding one—or contemplate setting up your own small business. Enrol at evening classes. Join clubs. There is a chance that you will view your husband in a different light when other aspects of your life have changed and maybe he will see you differently as your life flourishes. There is even a chance that your husband may be less likely to take you for granted when he sees you changing into a butterfly.

On the other hand, I must warn you that by changing your life you may antagonise your husband. If he likes his life the way it is—and feels comfortable having you around to ensure a constant supply of hot meals and clean socks—then he may feel threatened and become even more of a pain. The consolation is that if this happens you'll be in a much better position to pack your bags and wave him goodbye.

....

PORK PIES

Both my doctor and my dentist say you aren't a proper
doctor. My doctor says you never finished medical school.
If they're right why do you call yourself 'doctor'?

Your doctor and your dentist are both telling pork pies
and will never go to heaven. I have three degrees and
practised as a general practitioner in the Midlands for ten
years. Over the years I've made a lot of enemies by attacking
drug companies and the medical establishment. My critics
often find it easier simply to tell lies and to dismiss me as
'unqualified' than to try to deal with what I write.

Every week I receive a fistful of letters from confused
readers who tell me that their doctors have dismissed me,
this column and my claims and campaigns as dangerous
and irrelevant nonsense.

So, just to put the record straight, here are just twenty of
the scores of assertions and predictions I've made in the
past which were regarded as controversial, iconoclastic and
even heretical at the time (and which attracted varying
degrees of derision and vitriol from the medical establishment) but which are now widely accepted by the majority of
other doctors.

1. When I wrote that stress and tension could cause
high blood pressure, one professor wrote to say that if I'd
been a student of his he would have failed me. Today most
doctors accept that stress is a notable cause of high blood
pressure.

2. My initial warnings about mercury in teeth were
dismissed as 'scaremongering'. Today, many doctors and
dentists share my fears.

3. When, in the 1980s, I forecast that the number of old
people in our society would soon be so great that doctors
and hospitals wouldn't be able to cope the fears were
dismissed. Recent evidence shows that the fears were
entirely accurate.

4. My opposition to the fluoridation of water was widely

opposed. Today a growing number of experts believe that adding chemicals to drinking water can be hazardous.

5. Everyone sneered when I said that laughter could help improve health.

6. My enthusiasm for TENS machines for relieving pain was for years opposed by doctors and drug companies alike.

7. When I advocated the decriminalisation of drugs I was attacked as a dangerous lunatic. Recently politicians supporting my campaign used information I had unearthed to help substantiate a call for a Royal Commission.

8. My predictions that tuberculosis and plague were both coming back were dismissed as nonsensical. Now it is clear that both diseases *are* coming back.

9. It was several years after my condemnation of the condition of our water supplies before other critics agreed with me.

10. My warnings about Mad Cow Disease have for years been dismissed by the establishment as dangerous nonsense. But the evidence supports my claims.

11. When I first suggested that electricity might cause cancer, I was attacked.

12. The Government eventually admitted that it had acted over tranquillisers because of my articles. And nearly all doctors now agree with me that tranquillisers and sleeping tablets should not be prescribed for long periods. But when I first started campaigning about tran-quillisers almost the entire medical establishment attacked me, claiming that these drugs were safe.

13. When I produced evidence showing that AIDS was not a major threat to heterosexuals I was viciously attacked.

14. Exercise freaks condemned my warning that too much exercise could be hazardous. Today just about everyone agrees I was right.

15. My claim that female hormones in drinking water are affecting male babies is now widely supported. At the time I first made the claim, it was dismissed as nonsense.

16. The warnings I made about passive smoking were attacked for years. Today many doctors have joined the campaign for smoke free air in public places.

17. A dozen years ago I warned about the dangers of allowing children to watch video nasties.

18. My warnings that the government was trying to cut costs by releasing patients from long stay mental institutions were regarded as unjustifiably cynical for years.

19. Many years after I had shown how hospital administrators were wasting billions of pounds officials agreed with me.

20. On numerous occasions specific drugs which I have attacked have been withdrawn from the market.

....

DANGEROUS APPLIANCE

I am a divorced lady of 67 years. I am not in good health. Recently a close friend bought me a vibrator which has given me no end of pleasure and fulfilment. I have been told that these appliances are dangerous and not intended for insertion. What is the truth?

Make sure you use plenty of lubricant, don't push your vibrator in far enough to cause you any pain and take care not to let go of it. When I worked in a hospital casualty department I once saw a female patient who had a buzzing inside her. When I eventually succeeded in catching hold of, and removing, a small vibrator (complete with long lasting batteries) she attempted to deal with her embarrassment by expressing surprise and insisting that she had never seen the device before. When I had washed the vibrator I offered it to her but she refused it, saying that it wasn't hers. She was staying in a nearby hotel and she claimed that the vibrator, which she said must have been left in her bed by a previous visitor, had probably snuck inside her while she was asleep. I am proud of the fact that I showed no obvious signs of disbelief when she told me this.

CLIMBING THE CHRISTMAS TREE

I am a widower and very fit. My hobby is gardening. There is a small factory next to my home and one warm day recently the girls who work there exchanged light hearted banter with me as they ate their lunches on the grass. I offered them drinks of tea and later two of the girls came into my garden to bring back the mugs. I was in my shorts and they started teasing me. Things got out of hand and one of the girls ran her hand up my shorts. She received quite a shock since my member is over 12 inches long and has a girth of more than 7 inches. The other girl wanted to look and so we went indoors. Then one thing led to another. It has now become regular practice for some of the girls to come into my home and 'climb the Christmas tree' as they call it. I never thought that women could get so excited by giving themselves pain. They taught me many things—including oral sex. Several of the women now take turns to visit me in the evenings too. I am worried about the possibility of fathering a child. Would this be possible at my age? I feel very guilty about my lapse into libidinousness but I find these assignations difficult to resist. Do you think I am a 'dirty old man'? Should I seek advice to help me conquer these newly aroused urgings?

No, I don't think you're a dirty old man at all. A lucky old man, maybe. But not dirty. It would be perfectly possible for you to father children and so I suggest you buy a large boxful of condoms and use them both to reduce the chances of finding yourself surrounded by unwanted offspring and to limit your own exposure to sexually transmitted diseases. Then I suggest that you build a small altar in your living room and give thanks every evening to the kindly god who endowed you so generously and then put the factory at the bottom of your garden. With these nubile nymphets perched precariously on top of your Christmas tree you have provided adequate proof that there are at least fairies at the bottom of someone's garden.

A BIG MISTAKE

You recently wrote about being at medical school in the 1840s. Surely this was a big mistake?

No, it was a small joke.

GRATEFUL

After I read one of your articles I realised that many of the symptoms I had were being caused by the pills I was taking. I discussed this with my doctor who reluctantly agreed that I could stop the pills and see what happened. My symptoms disappeared within a week and I now feel a thousand per cent better. I am very grateful to you. More people should be aware of the potential hazards involved in taking drugs they might not really need.

Four out of every ten patients taking prescription drugs suffer side effects—many of which are potentially life threatening. And yet there are still many doctors who either don't know or don't care about this. In the same post as your letter I received a letter from a reader telling me that her doctor had taken a cutting of this column from her, angrily ripped it up and thrown it into her wastebasket—dismissing the information it contained as 'scary rubbish'!

UNATTRACTIVE PUBIC HAIR

My husband loves me but he has lost interest in sex because my pubic hair has become thin and unattractive. We used to have great sex. What can I do?

I think a wig is likely to be pretty unmanageable so why not just shave the stuff off completely? Many men would find such a prospect extremely exciting—especially if you livened up the immediate environment with a pair of sexy panties, a suspender belt and a pair of black seamed stockings.

FIVE MINUTES

I recently visited my GP for the first time in 18 months. I had hardly sat down and started to describe my symptoms when the doctor, who had been scribbling on the previous patient's medical records, looked up and told me that I'd only got five minutes so would I please hurry up. Is it now official NHS policy for patients to be allowed only five minutes at each consultation?

Your doctor probably had an urgent appointment at the local golf course, hairdresser or beauty salon. British GPs spend an average of about *eight* minutes with each patient. This compares badly with patients in other countries. Patients get 10 minutes in the USA; 12 minutes in New Zealand, 15 minutes in Canada and 21 minutes in Sweden. I heard of one surgery in the north where patients are alleged to have to make separate appointments for each symptom. Some doctors work such long, hard hours that they make themselves ill. Others rush through their work and spend a total of no more than a few hours a week with their patients. I suspect you've got one of the duds. Dump her.

GELATIN

Is it true that capsules are made of gelatin—an animal compound? I am a vegetarian and worried by this.

Yes. Most capsules are currently made from gelatin. But it is perfectly possible to make capsules from vegetable cellulose. Drug companies will only do this when they get enough letters from patients protesting about their continued use of gelatin capsules. It is up to you to help change things.

CURING A SIX YEAR ITCH

I have been married for six years. My marriage was getting very stale and even when I walked around naked I couldn't turn my husband on. Then I spoke to a friend who suggested that I wear sexy stockings and frilly knickers. I didn't want to do this at first because I felt rather embarrassed but eventually I did and I could not believe the difference it made. Now our sex life is wonderful and our marriage is much healthier.

I suggest that you thank your friend for alerting you to the most important secret of sexual happiness. Many marriage experts would be out of business if doctors were given permission to prescribe black stockings, lacy suspender belts, silky camisole tops, peek-a-boo bras and entirely impractical panties. These things would do far more good than most of the expensive tranquillisers, sleeping tablets, antidepressants and other pharmaceutical junk on the market. Politicians should be actively campaigning for VAT to be taken off impractical lingerie and put on the boring, sensible stuff.

It used to be said that the way to a man's heart was via his stomach. Forget that. A woman can take a man anywhere she wants with a lead made of a couple of feet of elastic and a few square inches of something skimpy.

STILL A VIRGIN

I am 17 and although I have had several boyfriends I am still a virgin. After I have been out with someone for a few months I get bored with them. For the last eighteen months I have found some women as attractive as men and have wondered if I could be a lesbian. I needed to talk to someone so I mentioned this to my best friend. She thinks that I have been brainwashed by the fact that most of my favourite singing artists are gay. She refuses to talk to me about it. All my other friends hate homosexuals so I have no one else to talk to either. I know in my own mind that I have not been brainwashed and I am not afraid of the fact that I might eventually find that I am a lesbian or at least bisexual. I would like to meet people who think the same way that I do but I don't know where to start. I thought about ringing a lesbian and gay telephone line I found but it is in London and my mum will go mad if there is a long distance call on our bill.

What's the rush? Take your time to explore your sexuality yourself. I agree that talking to committed homophobes is pointless but if you speak to committed lesbians then you'll still be getting biased advice and there is a risk that you may find yourself being talked into believing that you are a lesbian when you may not be. Once you start looking for advice you'll find lots of people prepared to give it to you.But objective, impartial advice is rarer than you might think.

Go to parties, join clubs and make as many new friends as you can—of both sexes. When you first find a partner you feel you want to go to bed with you'll start to learn what you really need to know about yourself. The only way you'll find the real truth about yourself is through experience.

WHEN A MAN IS A WOMAN

My 18-year-old son says he wants to be a girl. I was brought up to believe that a man is a man and a woman is a woman. I am very sad to think that my son is a little fairy. I'm sure that as a doctor you will agree with me that an 18-year-old boy should not wear make up, dresses, skirts, stockings and high heels. He does this nearly all the time. The only thing in his favour is that he certainly looks good in feminine clothes. He has got a job and goes to work dressed as a woman. The people he works with are completely taken in by him. One of them said what a lovely daughter I have. What shall I do? Do you think my son is a transvestite?

It sounds to me as if your son is more likely to be a trans-sexual than a transvestite. There is an important difference.

Transvestitism—or cross dressing—is practised by thousands of entirely heterosexual men and women who get pleasure or relief from stress and tension by dressing in clothes usually regarded as more appropriate to members of the other sex. Virtually every healthy, sane, sensible woman in the country is a transvestite for most wear jeans and trousers from time to time without thinking anything of it. They certainly aren't accused of being homosexual or perverted. Male transvestites have a harder time. They are, however, essentially male, usually enjoy making love to women and don't want to change sex. Unlike using drugs and alcohol to combat stress, dressing in camisoles, French knickers, stockings and suspenders and frocks is an entirely harmless activity.

Transsexuals (who are less common than transvestites) are men or women who feel trapped in the wrong bodies. Transsexual men feel that they should have been born as women. And transsexual women feel that they should be men.

Try to understand your son. He really needs your support. Talk to him. Ask him whether he thinks he is a transsexual or a transvestite.

If he is a transvestite then there is no need to seek any outside help. Many transvestites are better balanced (psychologically) than non-transvestites.

If your son is a transsexual—and genuinely wants to become a woman (rather than occasionally dress as one)— he may eventually want to make what he feels are necessary (and permanent) physical adjustments to his body. The first step towards this end will involve an appointment with a (hopefully) sympathetic psychiatrist. Your GP should be able to find the name and address of someone with experience in this area.

WET DREAM

Last night I had a wet dream. I dreamt that I was making love to one of the weather girls off the television. It is a long time since I had sex and it was wonderful—even if it was only a dream. I dreamt that the girl performed oral sex on me and it was terrific. How can I make sure that I have another dream like this?

There is no way to guarantee a repeat performance but you can increase your chances of success by making sure that you are thinking about a suitable weather girl as you drop off to sleep. There are, as far as I am aware, no laws against this yet though I expect that the politicians are working on it so don't tell anyone else your secret.

FAT FRIEND

I suffer from arthritis and my doctor has told me that I should lose weight. He says that according to the official height/weight tables I am 8 stones overweight. However, I have recently seen several TV programmes and magazine articles in which people have said that it is all right to be fat. A friend, who is also overweight, says that dieting is just a sexist philosophy promoted by companies selling slimming products.

In my view the 'fat is beautiful' philosophy is nothing more than flummery and wishful thinking. I find the sight of really fat individuals trying to kid themselves that they are merely curvy, plump and cuddly more than just sad. When fat folk like your friend try to drag others into this self deluding fantasy world then I feel that they are behaving recklessly, dangerously and irresponsibly.

It is fair enough for people who are just one or two stones overweight to be fairly relaxed about their excess weight. But I think that anyone who tries to convince you that carrying *over 100 pounds* of unwanted fat is normal,

healthy and natural must either have the sort of intellectual fire power normally associated with lichen or is
exhibiting major skills in self delusion.

Your choices are simple. If you carry on being fat your
arthritis will cause you much pain and you'll probably end
up a disabled and deteriorating wreck within a year or two.
If you lose weight and reduce the pressure on your joints
you will probably find that you can get around much more
easily: your arthritis won't go away but it will almost
certainly cause you less trouble.

The choice is yours.

....

MIXED

I am a single woman. I recently had to go into hospital and
was shocked to find myself on a mixed ward. Most of the
other women were unhappy about this. The nurses said
they didn't like it. And one or two of the men seemed
embarrassed. Why do hospitals do this? I found it offensive and degrading and although I need another operation
I have made my mind up that I will not go into hospital
again.

Any hospital which puts men and women on the same
ward must be run by administrators who think of
patients as throughput consumables, inconvenient tumour
ridden glands and malfunctioning organs, rather than
real, live, breathing, eating, sleeping, farting, feeling individuals. People who are ill get better quicker when they are
relatively happy and contented (and as stress free as
possible). Anxiety and embarrassment make things worse.
At the best of times, even the most sympathetically run
hospital must, by its very nature, provide an alien, uncom-
fortable environment. Bright lights, antiseptic smells and
church-like hush all add to the stress of hospitalisation.
Putting men and women on the same ward is thoughtless,
stupid and uncaring. Sensitive members of both sexes find
such wards enormously disturbing. The insensitive and

boorish are merely likely to take advantage of the situation and increase the embarrassment endured by the sensitive.

I fear that all this is a symptom of the undisguised contempt with which many administrators seem to regard the patients who pay their grossly inflated salaries. If hospital administrators had to use ordinary hospital facilities when they were ill, they wouldn't dream of putting men and women on the same ward.

If other currently healthy readers think they would find it embarrassing to be on a hospital ward with members of the opposite sex I urge them to complain today to their local politician. Don't wait until you have to go into hospital. It will be too late then. Remember: *if you know of an injustice but do not complain about it before that injustice affects you, then you have no right to complain when it does affect you.*

No ENERGY

My boyfriend is very keen on physical fitness and spends all his time exercising. He never has any energy left for me. I enjoy sex very much and get very frustrated when I don't get it.

Thanks for the letter, the suggestion and the photo. Wednesday is fine. I'll bring the condoms. (This is called reader servicing. What other newspaper columnists offer this sort of facility?)

APOLOGISED

At a recent party a woman who was, I thought, my best friend said some terrible things to me. She has apologised and now says she had too much to drink. I miss having her friendship.

Try to forget and forgive. If you can't do both then try to do one.

FIVE INCH HIGH HEELS

My husband and I have been married for twelve years and although we both still love each other very much our sex life has been rather low key for quite a while now. Last Wednesday it was our anniversary and my husband suggested that we try something he had read about in one of your books. I dressed up in the tartiest clothes I could find (five inch heeled shoes, see-through white blouse, black bra, stockings and suspenders and an obscenely short black skirt) took a taxi into town and sat at the bar of our biggest and smartest local hotel. Twenty minutes later (after I had rejected the advances of two complete strangers who had obviously assumed that I was what I looked like) my husband, who had arrived earlier and had been watching, came and sat down beside me and started to chat me up as though he'd never met me before. After I'd 'let' him buy me dinner and we had flirted with one another outrageously he drove me to a quiet spot and we made love in the back of the car. It was the best sex we'd had for years. The following day a good friend of mine, clearly shocked, telephoned to tell me that she had seen my husband with a hooker. 'The funny thing was,' she said, 'that the woman looked a bit like you. But you should have seen the way she was dressed!' It took me a quarter of an hour to persuade her that the hooker was me! Anyway, I just wanted to thank you—and to let you know that your advice really worked for us.

Congratulations and thanks for letting me know about your successful night out. I've had so many similar letters recently that I'm now a little bit worried that hotel bars up and down the country may become completely clogged with happily married couples pretending to be hookers and tired businessmen—causing all sorts of problems for real hookers and tired businessmen. So, could you all please follow this simple rota system. People whose surnames begin with the letters A to D should try this simple sex game on Mondays. If your surname begins with the letters E to J your night is Tuesday. Wednesday is the night for people whose name begins with the letters K to N. Those of you whose name begins with O to S can go out on the town on Thursdays, and Fridays are for people with surnames beginning T to Z. We'll leave Saturdays and Sundays for the professionals. And take care. It's a good idea for him to get there before her so that he can make sure nothing gets out of hand.

••

TRANQUILLISERS

I was put on tranquillisers thirty years ago because I was suffering a lot from stress. I came off them five years ago. I still get nervy attacks. Do you think these could be a continuation of the withdrawal symptoms?

No, although I have been warning about the problems associated with these drugs for over twenty years I doubt if the symptoms you have got now are withdrawal symptoms. Don't forget that you were originally given tranquillisers because you were having some sort of nerve trouble. The tranquillisers won't have cured you. Maybe you now need to learn to deal with your stress and anxiety more effectively.

••

BEAUTIFUL EYES

While travelling from London to York on a crowded train recently I found myself sitting next to a really terrific looking woman. She had beautiful eyes, a magnificent figure and a great sense of humour and we got on extremely well. By the time we got to Leicester we were holding hands. At Derby I'd got my arm around her and we were kissing and cuddling like long time lovers. After the train pulled out of the station at Sheffield we made love in one of the loos. I had to get out at York but she was going on to Newcastle. I nearly stayed on the train with her and now I wish I had. She wouldn't give me her name, address or telephone number but I can't get her out of my mind. What can I do?

I know I'll probably never see her again but I can't forget her wonderful laughing eyes and her soft, ripe body.

Why should you want to forget her? Enjoy the sweet memory. Keep each moment fresh in your mind and try to remember your on board love affair as an entirely perfect romance, never spoilt or threatened by the harshness of reality and untouched by any disappointment, frustration or regret. Dreams and memories are there to protect you from the dull and savage days. Don't let such a perfect adventure fade; guard it, put it away and take it out when the skies are grey with oppressive thunderclouds. In due course you will, I hope, find a partner with whom you can develop a more permanent, lasting, loving romance. Meanwhile, you have touched love and that is more than some people achieve in a lifetime.

Is this true?

My boyfriend says that if we have sex in the middle of a period then I cannot get pregnant. Is this true?

Most women ovulate—and are therefore at their most fertile—midway between their menstrual periods. Since you can't get pregnant unless an egg and a sperm get together you are extremely unlikely to get pregnant if you have sex during a period but I am too old to believe that anything is impossible.

Polish and proud of it

My son is changing his name. I am Polish and proud of it. How can I persuade him that what he is doing is dishonouring his family.

If your son wants to change his name because he is ashamed of his background and family then I can see that you've got problems, but maybe he is proud of being

Polish but fed up of all the aggravation that goes with having a name that looks as if it was created by a cat walking on a typewriter keyboard. Maybe he reckons that life will be easier if he doesn't have to spend 5 minutes every day repeating his name, spelling it and getting indignant with people who insist on pronouncing or spelling it wrongly. If he wastes just 5 minutes a day like this (and that is probably a conservative estimate if you've got one of those major misprint names with no vowels and lots of consonants) then that, in a lifetime, that will add up to a waste of *ten weeks!* Talk to him and ask him *why* he wants to change his name.

....

NOT MY TYPE

A man I work with, and whom I have always got on well with, asked me to go out with him. I said 'no', as gently as I could. I explained that I have a boyfriend and added that though I liked him as a friend he was not really my type. Since then he has made my life a misery. He has started spreading a rumour that I'm a lesbian and just sniggered and didn't deny it when I accused him of sending me anonymous letters and making late night anonymous telephone calls.

You need to squeeze the pus out of this malevolent human carbuncle immediately. Gather as much evidence as you can to support your complaint and then tell your boss exactly what has happened. Make it clear to the carbuncle itself that if his petty and irritating campaign continues you will also report him to the police and have him permanently lanced. And then do your best to ignore him. Try to resist the temptation to retaliate by starting slanderous rumours of your own ('he trained as a social worker, votes Conservative, spends his weekends train spotting and is very dull in bed') since this will encourage him to believe that you recognise his miserable existence.

....

UGLY AND STUPID

Seven years ago my parents divorced and I chose to go and live with my father and my stepmother. I had never really got on very well with my mother. When I was a child she was always telling me that I was ugly and stupid. My older brother stayed with my mother. After two years my brother told me that my mother was having a nervous breakdown. He said it was my fault because she felt that I had rejected her. Reluctantly, I went back to live with her. We immediately started having rows. She constantly said hateful things about me, my father and his new wife and all my friends. Three boyfriends broke up with me because they couldn't cope with her. It soon became clear to me that my mother only wanted me living with her to score points off my father. So I left home and moved into a bedsit. Now my brother tells me that my mother is crying all the time because I've left. She rings me up all the time and pretends to miss me but I know that she's putting it on in order to trick me into returning. I really don't want to go back. I don't think I have the strength to cope with her any more. Even though she is my mother and I know I should love her I am afraid that she is a very spiteful and manipulative woman. She will never admit that she is wrong and she never lets other people live their own lives. She seems to get real pleasure out of interfering and destroying. I feel guilty for feeling this way.

If a friend told you this story you would advise her to stand firm, wouldn't you? You would, I suspect, tell her that she should wave a metaphorical (or maybe even a real) two fingers at her mother.

We all have more freedom in our relationships with our relatives—and, indeed, others whom we love—than we do with acquaintances and strangers. With people who are close to us we can get away with things that would never be allowed in most other relationships. We can be rude and brutally honest in a way that would cause permanent damage to any less well founded relationship.

But that freedom carries with it extra responsibility.

Because we can be tougher and more honest with our relatives—and can reasonably expect their love to make them more forgiving and understanding of our faults and peccadilloes—we have a responsibility to be more sympathetic and compassionate.

Your mother has, it seems, taken all the rights that motherhood gives her and yet refused to acknowledge the responsibilities.

I think you should tell her to piss off and leave you alone. Your strength and determination may help her to see what a nasty old bitch she is. But somehow I doubt it.

EFFEMINATE LOOKS

I have very effeminate looks. Many people think I am gay but I am not. Is it possible for me to take hormones that will make me look more manly? I know that some female athletes who take steroids eventually start to look like men so maybe I should take some of those. Where can I get them?

Forget about taking hormones. I know of no safe way in which you can change your physical appearance without endangering your health. So declare your masculinity in other ways; the clothes you wear, the way you walk, the way you talk and so on. And try to stop worrying about what other people think about you. The people you care about will know the real you. And console yourself with the knowledge that while it is true that some women like men with huge biceps and hairy chests, there are many more who value humour and romance far more highly.

A MISTAKE

When my sister visited her doctor's surgery recently she was handed my medical records by mistake. She noticed that the doctor had written SCHIZOPHRENIC on the top of the records envelope and has now told all the members of my family. I have never been told that I am schizophrenic and I now feel very depressed about this. There has been a change in the way my family treat me.

Doctors are sometimes very cavalier about the things they write on patients' medical records. I once heard of a GP who wrote PSYCHOPATH on the top of the medical records of anyone he didn't like. By the time he retired he had learnt to dislike over a third of his practice and the label had become a bit of a joke. But I bet it wasn't much of a joke when patients moved away to other parts of the country and found the PSYCHOPATH label accompanying them.

Your doctor's staff were wrong to let your sister see your medical notes and your sister was wrong to report what she had seen to the rest of the family. But it may well be that your doctor (or whoever did it) was wrong to write the word on your medical records.

I suggest that you urgently make an appointment to see your doctor and that you discuss things with him. Tell him what has happened and ask him to explain.

For years I have campaigned for patients to be able to keep their own medical records at home. Your rather sad story is just another reason why this would be the right thing to do.

POINTLESS AND ENDLESS WORRYING

I worry a lot about little things which, in my heart, I know do not matter very much. When I send someone a present I worry about whether or not they'll like it. Whenever I put down the telephone I find myself worrying about whether I might have said something out of place. All this worrying is wearing me out. How can I stop this pointless and endless worrying?

You have to learn to get your worries into perspective. First, try to think your worries through to the bottom line. What is the worst that is going to happen if someone doesn't really like a present they get? Try this. Next time you find yourself worrying about something ask yourself how important the worry will seem in ten years' time. You'll almost certainly realise that the worry will have no significance in ten years time. Then ask yourself how important the worry will be in a year's time or a month's time. You should soon be able to differentiate between real worries—which are likely to have an impact on your life—and superficial worries which have no real importance. And you'll probably be liberated enormously when you find that most of the things you spend most of your time worrying about aren't worth worrying about at all. Once you've managed to get rid of all the trivial worries, you can spend your time worrying about the things that really matter.

··

GLUE LIKE

I've been dating my current boyfriend for four weeks. He enjoys me masturbating him but his semen is very thick and glue like. It doesn't spurt out but just sort of sits on the end of his penis. All my previous boyfriends made quite a mess when ejaculating and this turned me on. Is there anything wrong with my boyfriend? Will he be infertile? Is there anything we can do to make his semen more runny?

Semen is usually sticky and creamy. It is thick immediately after ejaculation, then becomes more liquid and eventually dries after exposure to the air. (The white stain can usually be removed with a stiff brush and a weak solution of sodium bicarbonate. Semen stains are fluorescent under ultraviolet light, by the way.) The colour varies but is normally white, grey or yellow. The distance a man fires his semen varies and the world record is eight feet eight inches. This doesn't have much influence over his chances of becoming a father (though the ancient Hebrews used to believe that sperm which didn't come out forcefully wasn't fertile) since sperm can swim—and as long as they're deposited in the right general area they can make their way up into the womb by themselves.

There are several possible reasons for a change in a man's ejaculatory pattern. These include increasing age, diabetes, back injury and prostate trouble. Also, some drugs are known to have an effect on the amount of semen and the distance it travels after leaving the penis. Your boyfriend should have a word with his doctor.

USELESS IN BED

Jack, a friend of ours, recently separated from his wife and came to stay with us. He was very broken up about it. Things weren't made easy for him by the fact that his wife, who works at the same place as he does, had told all her friends that he was useless in bed. About a week after he had moved in the three of us were sitting in the living room watching a rather erotic late night movie when my husband quietly drew my attention to the fact that Jack had an enormous erection. Saying that he was going to make a cup of tea my husband then went out into the kitchen. While he was there he called to me to join him. He then reminded me that when we have been making love we have frequently fantasised about having a threesome. He asked me if I fancied making love to Jack. At first I was rather shocked at the idea of putting a fantasy into practice but when I thought about it for a moment I found the idea very exciting. The movie had turned me on and I have always found Jack attractive. I told my husband to stay where he was and went back into the living room where Jack was still watching the movie. I sat down beside him and after a few moments casually put my hand on his inner thigh. Jack was clearly surprised and looked at me and then at the door, obviously anxious in case my husband should reappear. I told him not to worry and asked him to kiss me. Five minutes later I was down to my bra and panties giving Jack a blow job when my husband walked back in. Because of the position I was in I didn't see him at first but could tell by Jack's reaction what had happened. I heard my husband tell Jack it was OK. I then felt him pull down my panties and enter me from behind. During the next two hours both men made love to me in every possible position, sometimes both together and sometimes one at a time.

You should have seen the delighted look on Jack's face when I told him that his wife was wrong about his sexual prowess. He moved out to his own flat two weeks later but still comes back to sleep with us once or twice a week.

It is at Jack's suggestion that my husband and I would now like to offer my services to any other man who lacks sexual confidence. Jack says that I gave him back his manhood and I feel that I could provide other men with a useful service. It would be a sort of social work because I would not charge any money. How do I set about doing this?

There are a few sexperts who provide patients with surrogate lovers and they might well be keen to take up your generous offer (though I fear that your husband's presence and assistance might be regarded as less welcome). Your doctor, local hospital or nearest university should be able to give you the names and addresses of local sex therapists.

But before you dedicate yourself wholeheartedly to waving your bum in the air to save the nation, might I suggest that you think a little more carefully about what you are getting yourself into?

By your own admission your first (and so far only) experience in this valuable area of human endeavour was inspired by nothing more complicated than an erotic movie, a visitor's impressive erection and a conveniently matching personal fantasy. The whole thing was made even more acceptable by the fact that you fancied your temporary partner.

How will you feel about removing your knickers to try and satisfy an impotent, underendowed, overweight, garlic breathed solicitor at 10.30 am on a Monday morning?

DO I NEED TO SCRUB MY NIPPLES?

I am five months pregnant and would like to breast feed my baby. My mother says I should start scrubbing my nipples with a toothbrush or nail brush in order to get them ready. My nipples are very sensitive. Do I really have to do this?

No. Nor do you have to hang kippers round your waist, massage vast quantities of clear honey into your breasts or stand on one leg singing arias from La Bohème.

MINE ARE BIGGER THAN HERS

A girlfriend and I recently compared our labia when we were in the showers. They seem quite different. Mine are much bigger than hers and rather darker in colour. Is this normal?

Yes. Sexual bits and pieces (of both varieties) are as unique as fingerprints. A friend of mine who is a gynaecologist swears he can identify all his patients by looking at what he calls the 'business end'. Another friend, who works with him as a nurse, confirms that he will often hurry into a clinic, glance at a patient lying flat on her back with her legs in the air, and then address her by name without so much as a glance at her face.

ER...

I am very indecisive. Is there anything I can do about it?

Probably not.

WILL MY PENIS STOP GROWING?

I am a 17-year-old boy. I always wear quite snug fitting, brief-style underpants. My girlfriend says these could damage my penis, restricting its growth. Is this true? Would I be safer if I wore boxer shorts?

The shape and style of your underwear is unlikely to have any positive or negative impact on your penis's growth prospects.

Short term growth is in your girlfriend's hands. Long term growth is in your genes.

AN EASY LIFE

My girlfriend won't argue with anyone about anything. She likes an easy life and always agrees with people. How do I get her to change?

You probably can't. But look on the bright side: her life will be so stress free that she'll probably live for ever. When an American recently celebrated his 105th birthday a reporter asked him for the secret of his longevity.

'I never argue,' said the man.

'That can't be all there is to it!' said the reporter, sceptically and rather aggressively.

The old man shrugged. 'Maybe you're right,' he said, without hesitating.

RICH PARENTS

I am dating a rather well to do young lady who has rich parents. When I'm invited round to dinner I try to put on a better speaking voice and always end up putting the letter H in front of lots of words. I hear myself saying things like: 'Dinner was habsolutely wonderful' and 'The weather has been hawful'. I'm sure they take the mickey out of me behind my back.

Be yourself. Take confidence from the fact that your girlfriend is going out with you because you are you. If she wanted to go out with a chinless, witless, hunting, shooting upper class twit with a plum in his mouth and a firm aubergine stuffed up his rear end, then she would presumably not be going out with you. You do not have to pretend to be something you are not. Indeed, such a pretence can only damage your chances of cementing your relationship—and making a good impression on her family.

Your confidence has been weakened by the fact that you have concentrated too much on your girlfriend's parents' wealth and too little on your own good points. Try to give your self assurance a boost by making a list of all your virtues, skills and accomplishments.

....

A TRANSVESTITE WRITES

I am a transvestite. I'm married and my wife knows about my transvestism and is very supportive. We sometimes shop together as sisters. Once every month I go out to a meeting of a transvestite group to which I belong. I was carefully driving home from a social evening the other night (wearing a split skirt, a pink blouse, five and a half inch heels, a shoulder length blonde wig and full make up) when my car suddenly stuttered to a halt. I had run out of petrol. I was horrified; as much at my own stupidity as at anything else. I was in a part of town that I don't know very well and there was no telephone box to be seen. I sat there for a moment or two wondering what on earth to do. I didn't think that things could possibly be worse. Then a police motor cyclist pulled up alongside me and I knew that they could. I was terrified. It is, I suspect, every transvestite's nightmare to be arrested while 'dressed'. I wound down the car window and said 'hello', trying to sound as feminine as I could. The policeman asked me what was wrong. When I explained he told me that there was a garage near by. He ordered me to wind up my window, lock the doors, stay in the car and wait. He then roared off out of sight. Less than five minutes later he was back clutching a can of petrol. He put the petrol in the car and I asked him how much I owed him. He smiled and said I didn't owe him anything but would I go for a drink with him one evening. I couldn't believe my ears. I know I look quite convincing and make a realistic woman when I'm 'dressed' but I'd never expected this. I can't remember exactly what I said—I was just desperate to get away—but I remember exchanging telephone numbers and now I'm terrified that he will ring. I just don't know what to say or do.

If he 'read' you and realised that you weren't quite what you appeared to be, then your over friendly policeman may have homosexual leanings and may wrongly assume that you have too. If he didn't 'read' you—and honestly thought you were a woman—then an evening out is likely to end in disappointment, anger and fairly considerable embarrassment.

Since you aren't homosexual and obviously don't want to embarrass your kindly saviour you have to get out of your date and let him down as lightly as you can. Waiting for him to ring you is likely dramatically to increase your chances of having a premature heart attack so the best bet must be for you to ring him and get this over as soon as possible. Try to think of something simple but final if you're going to lie. Telling your blue suited Don Juan that you have to rush off to nurse your ageing grandmother in the Orkneys could lead to all sorts of unwanted complications and leave you taking part in an unpleasantly realistic French farce. Your best bet is to tell him that you're married (that bit, at least, is true) and that although you found him enormously attractive you've thought it over and you really don't think a meeting would be a good idea. Be firm. If he says he just wants to be friends tell him that you found him too attractive for that. Thank him again for his kindness and ask him if you can send him cash to cover the cost of the petrol he bought for you. And next time you go out 'dressed' do make sure you fill your petrol tank beforehand!

A YEAR OFF

My daughter has got a place at university to study modern languages but she wants to take a year off before she starts her studies. I think she should continue with her education and have a year off when she's finished her degree course. What do you think?

Your daughter will find it difficult to settle down to academic studies if she takes a year off now. Much of university life will seem childish and banal after twelve months' contact with the real world. But if she waits until she has finished her degree course to take time off, the problems will be even greater.

I spent a year doing voluntary work in between leaving school and going to university and it was the most valuable educational experience I ever had. I learned more about people and life in that short period than I did in twenty years of formal education.

EXERCISE BORES ME

I want to get fit but exercise bores me. Is there any way to get fit without jogging, playing ball games or prancing around in a leotard?

Why not fuck your way to fitness? Sex is an excellent and under-estimated way to get into shape. Careful selection of positions should enable you to exercise just about every muscle in your body with the possible exception of those responsible for eyebrow movement—though come to think of it, if you surprise one another enough you could even give the eyebrows a workout. And you can burn up as many calories having sex as you can while jogging.

∙∙

NO SCRUPLES

My boyfriend is Jewish and a meat eater. I am vegetarian.
He claims that the way the Jews kill animals is humane. Is
he right?

No. His scruples are as abundant as his foreskin.
Animals killed for Jews have their throats cut while
they are fully conscious. Cows can take up to six minutes to
die so that your boyfriend can eat kosher meat. Incidentally,
I'm told that when they get up in the morning the first
thing Jewish men do is thank God that they weren't born as
women? Nice, eh?

∙∙

VERY MUCH IN LOVE

My girlfriend and I are both 18 and very much in love. We
plan to marry early next year and my girlfriend's parents
have already started to make the arrangements. We have
a wonderful sex life but neither of us has had any experience with any other partners. Recently my girlfriend asked
me if I had ever wondered what it would be like to make
love to another woman. When I admitted that I had, she
said that she had wondered what it would be like to go to
bed with a different man. I've talked to a couple of friends
about this and they both say that I should sow some wild
oats fairly quickly before I get married and it is too late.
However, although I am keen to do this I am not so keen
about my fiancée having sex with other men. I now don't
know what to do. I am worried that if I resist these urges
now I may find myself succumbing after I am married.

Abandon your plans for an early wedding. Cancel the
cake maker, the dress and the hotel booking. I don't
think that either you or your girlfriend are ready for
marriage yet. You don't have to abandon all ideas of
marrying one another. But you would be wise to put matri-
mony on ice for the time being. Neither of you are old
enough or mature enough to take such an enormous step.

The absence of a firm date for a wedding will free you both to enjoy one another and will remove this feeling that you urgently need to do a little more sexual exploring before you settle down. Concentrate on having fun and starting to grow old together and see what happens. You will either grow closer together or you will grow apart. If you grow closer together then make another date for your wedding. You'll enjoy the occasion far more. If you grow apart it will be painful but you will at least be able to do it without bloodsucking lawyers wrecking what is left of your relationship and taking all your money.

....

WHIRLWIND ROMANCE

I work as a presenter for a local radio station. A few months ago I got married to a girl I had met while opening a shop in the town where I work. She worked as an assistant in the store and I fell in love with her immediately. It was a whirlwind romance and we married less than three months after we had met. You will probably be surprised to hear that sexually speaking I was very inexperienced when I got married. I had only had three previous girlfriends and had been to bed with only one of them. It never occurred to me that my wife might be considerably more experienced than I was. Two weeks ago I came off air to find a group of other presenters, engineers and secretaries laughing at something. Naturally, I went over to see what was amusing them. One of the other presenters immediately showed me what they were looking at—a section headed 'Readers' Girlfriend' in a several-years-old men's magazine. The page contained several nude photographs of my wife.

Shocked, I tore the magazine out of his hand and rushed to the store where my wife still works. I dragged her out to the car and took her home. She confessed that she had posed for the pictures when going out with another man. When I asked her straight out how many men she had been to bed with she told me that she couldn't remember but that

she thought it was probably seven or eight! She wouldn't
stop crying but kept insisting she loved me. I immediately
moved out and am now living with my mother. I miss her but
how can I ever go back to her knowing what I know?

I never fail to be impressed by the enormous reservoir of
kindness with which the human race is endowed. What
good friends you've got at the radio station. What jolly
chums they are to have torn your life into shreds for the sake
of a quick laugh. It isn't your wife you should be cross with
but the malevolent, evil spirited morons you work with.

Try to forget what your wife did before she met you. If she
really loves you, then nothing she did before she met you
matters. Her sex history is certainly not important (I am
assuming that both of you have been checked and that
neither of you contracted any diseases during your pre-
marital adventures). Lots of people do silly things when
they're young—but that doesn't mean that they are evil,
amoral or incapable of true and lasting love. Your wife's
sexual history is neither unusual nor exotic. Haven't you
ever done anything of which you are now rather ashamed or
embarrassed? Parked on a double line? Gone through traffic
lights on amber? Voted Conservative? Taken up a disabled
parking space at the airport? Fantasised about the political
figure of your choice being slowly ground into mince by a
shoal of uncontrollable, disenfranchised octogenarians?

I suggest that you buy the biggest bunch of flowers you
can afford and go home. Explain that you were hurt and ask
your wife to forgive your impetuosity. Curse the nasty little
pustules who caused you both so much pain and then repair
your bruised marriage with kisses, hugs and whatever else
comes naturally.

• •

MY HERNIA

I have a hernia and need surgery. The first surgeon to
whom my GP referred me has a waiting list of between
eighteen months and two years. After talking to a secretary

at the hospital he then found another surgeon who had a waiting list of just six weeks. Why isn't the incompetent surgeon with the two year waiting list disciplined? If it wasn't for the hard working surgeon with the short waiting list I would have had to wait much longer for my operation.

But how do you know that it is the surgeon with the long waiting list who is incompetent? Maybe the surgeon with the short waiting list has a short waiting list because most GPs refuse to send him their patients. Maybe he's an incompetent buffoon and the other surgeon—the one with the long waiting list—gets ten times as many patients to deal with.

I quite agree with you that hospital consultants should be assessed. And I agree that incompetent or inefficient specialists should be disciplined or sacked. But waiting times alone are not a good way of assessing consultant quality.

DROOPING BREASTS

I'm only 22 but my breasts, which are quite large, are already beginning to droop. Is there anything I can do to keep them firm and stop them sagging any more?

You can't make DD size breasts defy gravity and stick straight out but do the right sort of exercise and wear the correct bra and you can delay the rate at which even the largest breasts droop.

JELLY IN MY BRA

My little girl recently had a birthday party. After all the other children had gone home and my daughter had gone to bed my husband and I started to clear up. There was quite a lot of mess and a lot of food left over. My husband was nagging me about having made too much food when I don't know what came over me but I picked up a handful of blancmange and threw it at him. It landed right in the middle of his shirt front and I couldn't help giggling. He started to shout but then picked up a jelly, came across to where I was standing and pushed it down the front of my blouse and rubbed it into my bra and over my breasts. I then picked up a handful of trifle, undid his trousers and slipped it down inside his underpants. After a few minutes we were both covered in food. My husband undid my blouse and started licking the jelly off my breasts. I felt really sexy and knelt down and started eating up some of the trifle. In the past I've never been very keen on oral sex but licking the trifle off his penis really turned me on. A few moments later we were making love on the carpet. It was fantastic! There was a terrible mess to clear up but it was well worth it. Have you ever heard of anyone doing anything like this before?

You are by no means the first couple to discover the sexual delights of covering one another in food, licking some of it off and then humping through the resultant mess. Slippery, sticky, sweet foods such as custard, cream and syrup seem to be particularly popular with those who get their sexual kicks this way. Recently published, entirely unreliable research shows that 34.6% of the staff working for a major bank enjoy sexually stimulating food fights at least once a month. Oddly enough I've never heard of anyone getting turned on by a food fight with cold gravy or salted porridge (though now that I've said that I've absolutely no doubt that I will be flooded with letters from cold gravy and salted porridge aficionados).

....

GET FAT BY LOOKING AT FOOD

Is it possible to get fat just by looking at food? My mum swears she hardly ever eats and claims she only has to look at a cream cake to put on 5lbs!

You may be surprised to hear that your mum is right— it is possible to get fat simply by looking at food. When you see, smell or think of food your body starts to prepare its digestive processes. Saliva is released and your stomach juices get ready to digest the food it expects. Your pancreas will be stimulated to produce insulin and the insulin will start to convert the glucose in your bloodstream into fat because it anticipates more food coming in. As your blood sugar level falls so you'll feel genuinely hungry. And you'll eat. Even though you weren't hungry just a few moments earlier. The answer? Tell your mum to ban books and magazines that contain mouth watering pictures of food. And suggest that she wears blinkers when shopping trips are likely to take her past cake shops. (I'll lay evens some crafty entrepreneur is producing 'blinkers for slimmers' within a week.)

I FEEL FED UP

I sometimes feel very fed up. I am particularly fed up with people—most of whom are mean, gloomy, humourless hypocrites who think only about themselves.

I think you're right. The world is pretty well full of nasty bastards. I wouldn't mind terribly if the human race became extinct. Maybe it's time we gave some other creature a chance. I don't think ants, mice, cockroaches or termites could possibly make a worse job of things than we have. I certainly don't believe that any other creature has quite the reservoir of deceit that man has.

DOES COMPLAINING DO ANY GOOD?

I always complain when I buy shoddy goods but my husband says I shouldn't bother. He says I'll just get a reputation as a 'complainer' and that it won't do any good anyway.

You must complain. It is important. If we don't all complain when we buy lousy products and get shitty service then things will just get worse. (The Vernon

Coleman Guerrilla Army task for this week is to write at least one letter of complaint about an annoyance of your choice—something that you've bought and that has broken or isn't any good or some service you've paid for that has turned out to be not worth the money).

You should also try to remember to say something complimentary when you're pleased with goods you've bought or service you've been given. Drop the manufacturer, shop or individual concerned a short note of thanks or congratulations. You'll make their day and you'll feel good too.

PERFECTLY SAFE

I have been very nervy recently. My doctor gave me a prescription for tranquillisers. He said that they are perfectly safe to take for as long as I like. Is this true?

I know of no tranquilliser which can be safely taken indefinitely. I have been battling to persuade doctors that tranquillisers are addictive since 1973—that's over two decades ago! The government eventually acted (and admitted that they'd acted because of my articles) and I've lost count of the number of TV and radio programmes which were eventually made as a result of the campaign, but it seems that there are still some doctors around who haven't got the message. My advice is that if any doctor says any tranquilliser is perfectly safe you should run away from his surgery as quickly as you possibly can screaming 'Unclean! Unclean!' at the top of your voice.

A SMALL PROBLEM

I have a small problem which is far too trivial to bother my GP with (he is a very busy man). My tongue is slightly discoloured. Please advise. I will see my doctor if you think it worth his attention.

Put out your tongue. Move it to the left. Now to the right. Push it right out. Hmmmm. My word! Doesn't look good, does it? I don't think you should put that back into your mouth until you've let your own doctor have a look at it. Keep it out of your mouth and give it plenty of fresh air until your doctor has had a chance to examine it.

TWO GIRLS AND A DILDO

I'm 22 and recently changed jobs and moved to London where I now rent a room in a flat. The other two occupants of the flat, Jane and Karen, are girls in their mid twenties. They share the only other bedroom. My girlfriend was initially a little dubious about my sharing with two women but eventually accepted that the arrangement was purely one of convenience. I haven't had much to do with either of the girls because I often work late in the evenings and most weekends I go back up north to be with my girlfriend, but last Wednesday when the trains were on strike I accepted a lift from my boss and arrived back at the flat much earlier than I usually do. I walked into the living room and had the shock of my life when I saw Jane and Karen, who were both entirely naked, sprawled on the sofa watching a porno movie. They didn't seem in the slightest bit embarrassed. There was a dildo lying on the sofa between them. Jane offered me a glass of wine and neither of them made any attempt to cover up. It turned out that the two girls are lesbians and that although they have a rather 'loose' and uncommitted relationship they have been sleeping and living together for four years. Jane told me that she was bisexual but Karen admitted that her only sexual experience with a man had been such a disaster that she was really still a virgin. After we'd opened another bottle of wine Jane suggested to Karen that she ought to take advantage of the situation to find out what sex with a man—meaning me—was really like. At first I thought she was joking but realised she wasn't when she reached over, unfastened my trousers, took out my whatsit and started playing with it. I ended up making love to both of them and had the most amazing evening of my life. Afterwards we even slept together in their bed.

To my amazement the two girls seem to regard the evening as of no great significance. The following evening I asked Karen if she'd like to go out for a meal but she said that she was still a lesbian and not interested in a heterosexual relationship. I feel as though I've been used. I don't know whether to stay in the flat or move out and I don't know whether to tell my girlfriend or whether to keep quiet.

You will have to get used to the fact that after being used as a living, breathing dildo you have been discarded like an old condom (I hope you used condoms, by the way. If you didn't, then do pop along to your local Furtive Look Clinic and have your twiddly bits peeped at by experts in white coats who know about these things. Lesbians aren't immune to sexually transmitted diseases).

I don't think you should tell your girlfriend about your unsuccessful attempt to convert the natives. A confession might help you unload some of your guilt but it won't improve her life. If you can lock the memory of your orgiastic evening away in a little compartment under the heading 'Isolated Erotic Incidents' then stay in the flat. If you think you'll find that difficult to do, then you should start looking for accommodation elsewhere.

DAMPENED ENTHUSIASM

I get excruciating headaches whenever I have an orgasm. I don't get the headaches at any other time. As you can probably imagine this rather dampens my enthusiasm for sex (although I do like sex and the headaches are *not* a deliberate excuse!).

First, pop along and see your doctor for a check up. If he can't find anything wrong then you may be suffering from genuine 'sex' headaches. The explosive, violent, usually one sided headaches which sometimes accompany the moment of orgasm are a bit of a mystery but since such headaches are sometimes thought to be caused by over breathing you may be able to avoid them by making an effort to control your breathing during sex. Another possibility is that the headaches are a type of migraine.

· ·

AM I MAD?

I recently took a fairly low paid job with an organisation which does work which I respect. My father wants me to take a better paid job with the chemical company he works for. Do you think I'm mad to prefer to have less money but a job I feel good about?

Not at all. I am constantly amazed by the things which people are prepared to do for a living. Whatever you do I think you should try to spend your life doing things that *you* feel proud about. Personal respect is far more important than being able to afford new shag pile carpets and velvet wallpaper every 12 months.

· ·

MY BOYFRIEND'S FETISH

My boyfriend seems to have a fetish for girls wearing tight jeans. Whenever we go out he can't stop staring if he sees a girl's bum in denim. In the summer he wears dark glasses all the time and thinks I can't tell that he's staring but I can. Do you think he's a pervert?

No. He just suffering from a common medical disorder called Niceroundbumsintighttrousersgivemeahard-onitis. Other similar diseases include Bigbreastsinskin-tightsweatersmakemyeyespopoutitis and Lovelylonglegs-inveryshortskirtsmakemedriveintolamppostsitis.

No treatment is needed, which is just as well since none is available.

∙∙

I WANT PLASTIC SURGERY

I want plastic surgery to improve the shape of my nose but everyone thinks I'm potty. I've seen a picture of the nose I'd like. Do you think I'll be able to get the operation done?

As the owner of one of the largest noses in the galaxy I think you're pretty potty too. Why do you want plastic surgery? I bet you a pound that it isn't simply because you find your own nose aesthetically displeasing but because you think that having a new nose will change the way people look at you or think about you. And the chances are that it won't. Lots of people seem to regard plastic surgery as a potential miracle solution. I constantly get letters from girls wanting bigger breasts because they think that big breasts will change their lives. They won't. Having big tits doesn't make the owner immune to nastiness, spite, envy and small minded bigotry. After you've had the surgery the world will still be full of shitty people. Surgery won't make people suddenly start loving you and treating you decently. Wear the nose God gave you with pride. Hold your head up high and face the world with dignity and courage. Stuff anyone who doesn't like you because of the shape of your nose.

If you insist on having your nose reshaped you will, I'm sure, be able to find a surgeon prepared to deal with you.

∙∙

LET DOWN

At a meeting at work recently my boss criticised me at great length for something that was not my fault. He was so aggressive and so rude that I could not defend myself. People who I had previously thought of as friends all said nothing—even though they knew that the attack was quite unfair and unjustified. Afterwards two of these people came up to me and told me that they thought I had been treated unreasonably but confessed that they had not had the courage to stick up for me. One person said that he had tried to remain objective and impartial, another said he felt he had to be neutral. How do I still regard these people as friends? How can I have respect for them after they let me down so badly?

You've just learned the difference between true friends and passing acquaintances. Most people go through their lives afraid of speaking out and constantly living in fear of what might happen.

However frightened, stupid, faithless, selfish and vain you think people can be—you are wrong. People can be more stupid, more feckless, more vain, more selfish and more frightened than you could possibly imagine.

'Neutral', 'objective', 'fair' and 'responsible' are qualities which we are taught to admire. But, in truth, these are the qualities of the weak spirited and the passionless. Name me one great man who was ever 'fair'? Name me a social, technical or artistic advance produced by a 'bland' man.

....

TAKING CHARGE

My husband likes me to take charge when we have sex. If I loosely tie his wrists behind his back with my tights and gently whip his bottom with my best black bra he gets very excited and that turns me on. He likes me to wear boots, fishnet stockings and a tight, black, plastic micro skirt. Last Saturday there was nothing good on the TV and we were just getting into the swing of things in the living room when the door opened and my sister Daphne and her husband Harold walked in. My husband was stark naked, except for a pink, nylon baby doll nightie of mine which he likes to wear, and was bent over our beige leatherette sofa so he didn't see them arrive but I was in the middle of my back swing and saw them fling open the door. 'Surprise, surprise!' said Harold, who was brandishing a bottle of Tesco's claret. My thigh length plastic boots were still at the menders so I was wearing my black wellingtons which aren't really perfect but which are the only other boots I've got. There were a few little red lines across Harold's bottom so it was pretty obvious what I'd been doing.

Daphne is very straight laced and has been heard to say that people should only have sex when they want a baby (she and Harold have got one child and I think he was probably the result of their only sexual experience) and I honestly thought she was going to have a fit. Harold is a staunch member of the church choir, although I suspect that he probably keeps dirty magazines in the garden shed and he certainly didn't seem to mind looking at my bare breasts while Daphne was giving us both a piece of her mind. It rather spoilt the mood so we put our dressing gowns on, had a cocoa each and watched the fencing on television. The thing is, do you think we should stop what we do? We don't hurt anyone else and we both enjoy our little games.

I think you're both disgusting and should be thoroughly ashamed of yourselves. How dare you have fun with one another's bodies. Marriage is a sacred union and the human body should be treated as a temple. War, murder, deceit, tobacco production, over prescribing and corruption are insignificant moral crimes compared to the inappropriate wearing of feminine nightwear and the use of rubber boots as a substitute component of an erotic costume. Since your husband is clearly the ringleader he must be punished. Make him wear your baby doll nightie and kneel down in front of the sofa. Put on your boots and micro skirt and smack his plump, pink bottom till he pleads for more. Buy, beg or borrow one of those remote control cameras, take a picture of yourselves in action and use it to create a Christmas card to send to your anally constricted sister and her wretched husband.

Oh, and one other thing, if you're not going to lock the back door when you're giving impromptu performances you might as well get one of the neighbours to collect admission money.

A NIGHTMARE

My husband and I have just got back from a holiday in Spain. It was a nightmare. There were cats all over the place—all hungry and thirsty, some dying. We went out each morning and night taking food and water to them but couldn't carry enough food to feed them all. It broke my heart and I cried every day. I will never go back to Spain ever again. What can I do to help these poor creatures? I feel so helpless.

One can change some things with logical arguments and reasoned debates. Other things have to be changed by the judicious application of suffering. Naughty children sometimes only learn by being deprived of regular doses of television and I suspect that the Spanish will only start treating animals kindly when forced to do so through economic sanctions. Write to the Ambassador at the Spanish Embassy and tell him that you will never go back to his blood soaked country until his fellow countrymen start treating animals with respect. Spaniards are primitive, rather simple minded people who have few natural skills and rely entirely on their climate to make a living. But they have some native cunning and will start treating animals decently if they understand that the alternative is a boycott by holidaymakers. Economic boycotts helped win freedom for blacks in South Africa and will help win freedom for animals around the world.

TIMES ARE HARD

I am a married woman in my 30s. My husband is on a low wage and times are hard. We live in our own house with a mortgage but we need a new roof. We have saved some money but still cannot afford to have the whole job done properly. A friend has given us an estimate and suggested that we could make up the rest of the bill if I go away with him to a hotel for the night. My husband has no objection as our friend has had a vasectomy and does not have any infections. I find the whole idea very exciting but do you think this will hurt my relationship with my husband and our friend? Will this make me a prostitute? Do you think I will regret it? I would appreciate an early reply because our friend wants to start work on the roof in August.

You should think very carefully indeed before accepting your friend's offer. Technically, I suppose that if you go to bed with someone for financial gain (whether you get paid in cash, tins of pineapple or roofing tiles) then you are prostituting yourself. But I don't think that is the important point. Theoretically any woman who has been to bed with a man after he's bought her a meal—because she feels she ought to—is a prostitute. Anyone who has had sex with a partner out of gratitude for something else is a prostitute.

What matters—and you're obviously already worried about this—is what effect your night on the tiles is going to have on the rest of your life. Selling your body for part of a roof is bound to have an effect on your relationship with your husband (and your friend) and the big $69,000 question is: where is this all going to stop? Are you going to pay the window cleaner by giving him a hand job? What about a blow job for the local builder if the chimney needs repointing? Or are you only going to bed with the roofer because you fancy him? In which case, is once going to be enough?

NO MAN'S LAND

I am a transsexual. I was born male but have had an operation to change my sex. I did not do this lightheartedly. If I was Dutch or Danish or German I would now be entitled to be treated as a woman. But in Britain I am stranded in 'no man's land'—discriminated against at every turn. I have gone through much pain and anguish to become a woman. I now look like a woman. My friends believe I am a woman. I have had boyfriends who believed I was a woman. But I cannot marry. According to the law I cannot be raped. And I am at risk of being arrested for a 'breach of the peace' every time I go out of my front door. Why is Britain so backwards in acknowledging those of us who were born the wrong sex?

I share your concern and indignation. I don't like living in a backward country. So this week's task for members of the Vernon Coleman Guerrilla Army is to send the following letter of protest to their MPs: 'Why does Britain deny ordinary human rights to transsexuals? Do you not agree that individuals who have put up with enormous mental and physical anguish in order to change sex deserve to be taken seriously?'

....

A STUDENT NURSE

I am an 18-year-old male student nurse. I share a house with four girl students and about a month ago one of the girls (a muslim) told us that her brother was coming to the area for two weeks. She said that if he found out that she was sharing a house with a man she would have to go home. The other girls decided that I would have to become a woman while our friend's brother was around. They dyed my hair, lent me clothes and taught me how to use make up. I had never dressed as a woman before but I found it very exciting. I must have been convincing because my flatmate's brother asked me out and told me he wanted to make love to me. Even when I told him the truth he still insisted that he wanted me as his lover. In the end we went to a hotel and spent the night together. When he left the area he said that his sister could stay with us but that I had to forget all about him. I now miss him terribly and am very confused.

I'm not surprised that you are confused. You have, in the last few weeks, come face to face with two important and unexpected aspects of your own sexuality. I'm afraid I think you are probably going to have to accept the fact that your relationship with your flatmate's brother is over and was never anything more than a brief 'holiday' romance. (I hope you practised 'safe sex'. If you didn't or are in any doubt please visit a sexually transmitted diseases clinic straight away.) But you have to ask yourself whether your experiences with cross dressing and homosexuality were also transient or are of greater, longer lasting significance. Cross dressing and homosexuality do not usually go together—the vast majority of transvestites or cross dressers are interested only in having sex with real women—so I think you should try to separate these two experiences in your mind. Do you want to forget about cross dressing but experiment more with homosexuality? Do you want to forget about homosexuality but try cross dressing more often? Do you want to forget about both and return to being a 'straight' heterosexual? Or do you want to carry on cross dressing and find another boyfriend? The possibilities are almost endless if you want to mix and match and pick and choose between different aspects of your own sexuality.

WORTH THE EFFORT?

Is it really worth making the effort to write to politicians and newspapers? I sometimes feel that there is no point at all in ordinary people trying to change anything. The bureaucrats and the politicians just ignore us and carry on looking after themselves.

Things may seem bleak when your letters are continually ignored or when you receive yet another bland and meaningless response from a bland and meaningless politician but it certainly *is* worth making the effort. Who knows what the result will be? On 12th July 1789 an angry revolutionary called Camille Desmoulins jumped up onto a café table in Paris and made an impromptu, stirring speech which led, two days later, to the storming of the Bastille and the start of the French Revolution.

KIDNEY FOR SALE

I would like to sell one of my kidneys. Who can I write to?
I need the money for a flat.

However desperate you are, please forget about selling any of your organs in order to raise money. The Manufacturer gave you two kidneys because He thinks you need them. If you sell one you will invalidate the guarantee.

HAPPY HENS

I was recently shocked to discover that eggs sold as 'fresh from the farm' may have come from battery hens. I thought I was buying eggs from free range hens who had spent their lives happily scratching around in a farmyard. Would you please warn other readers of this.

Yes. When buying eggs ask the assistant to confirm that the eggs came from hens who were free to wander about and were *not* kept in cages.

I SHOOT BIRDS

I have an airgun and like shooting. I shoot birds, but because I don't want to risk hitting another person or breaking a window I never aim at birds when they are on the ground, only when they are in trees. My girlfriend has broken up with me. She says that what I am doing is cruel but she has a cat that kills birds and she still loves the cat— so why doesn't she love me?

The fact that the cat is obeying a simple, primitive hunting instinct designed to keep it alive—whereas you are a sadistic, psychopathic cretin getting your pleasure out of killing defenceless creatures purely for fun—may have something to do with it. Your girlfriend is obviously sensible and sensitive whereas you are simply an insensitive and intellectually deprived thug suited only to a career in politics or the pharmaceutical industry. I trust that your bank balance will always be small, that you will be for ever besieged by worries, uncertainties and guilt and that you marry an ambitious, pushy, razor tongued, ball busting, shopaholic feminist with halitosis, herpes and a moustache.

MY HUSBAND IS BORING

I am middle aged and married with two teenage sons. My husband is kind and thoughtful. He works hard, is popular and a lovely man. But I have recently realised that I find life with him boring. For several years now our sex life has been virtually non existent. A few months ago I started an affair with a young man who works in my office. He is not much older than my sons and I know there is no future in our relationship. But the sex is fantastic and I am enormously flattered that I can satisfy him. I have started masturbating again. I wear sexy clothes and I flirt with strangers. I had grown dull but I suddenly feel much more alive. Now I worry about getting older and want to make the most of the rest of my life. Should I leave my husband and try life alone? I don't know what is happening to me.

You're going through a mid life crisis—about as common among men and women in their 40s as spots are among teenagers. Your affair, probably triggered by boredom, has woken up your sleeping hormones and I'm afraid you're not going to find it easy to get them to shut up. Without regular sex your physical urges will have been hibernating. Now that you are back in your action your veins will be full of sex hormones. So now you've got to decide what you want to do with all your reawakened sexual energy.

First you must ask yourself whether you want your marriage to succeed. Do you want to awaken your husband from his sexual slumber? If you do then you must try—

stockings, lacy bra and perfume—and see what happens. If
you can't get him to show any interest at all, you have to
choose whether to sink back into dullsville and try to stuff
your hormones back into the box; decide that your relationship has reached its sell by date, leave and move into a
flat somewhere; or stay with him and continue having short
term but physically satisfying affairs. If you don't want to
awaken your husband's sexual urges because you don't
think of him 'that way' any more then that will presumably
tell you a good deal about your relationship.

Finally, remember that not all your new energy has to go
into humping. There is more to life than sex and orgasms.
Maybe you could harness a little of your energy and use it
to help do something you've always really wanted to do:
write a book, start a business, sail around the world single
handed or break the world disco dancing record.

I know all this is rather frightening but you may able to
take some slight comfort from the thought that there is one
thing worse than having a mid-life crisis: and that is *not*
having a mid life crisis but simply muddling along in
dullsville, unaware of your potential and dead from the
ankles up.

....

At the seaside

My wife and I recently took our two children on holiday to
the seaside. One of our children was hit on the side of the
head by a beachball. She was badly upset by the incident.
Will you help us organise a campaign to ban ball games
on beaches?

I don't think you're going anywhere near far enough. Ball
games are just the thin end of a very big wedge. Beaches,
parks and other play areas are potential death traps for
children. Children playing on sand or grass can fall, bang
their heads on small buckets, get wet feet in rock pools, be
hit on the head by falling kites and get sand up their noses.
As for swings and slides—well the potential for disaster is

vast. I really don't think your campaign goes anywhere near far enough. Indeed, I feel that by even allowing your children to play in public places you are demonstrating your unsuitability for parenthood. All decent and truly caring parents keep their children at home, wrapped up in cotton wool, bringing them out for display purposes only when close relatives arrive for tea.

....

SICK WITH GRIEF

My wife died two weeks ago. We were very much in love. I feel sick with grief. People just don't understand how I feel. They say 'get out and meet new people' and 'start a new life' and tell me that I have my grandchildren and my garden and so should be grateful. But my wife was my life and I miss her so much I just do not know what to do. I just sit in the house or walk around the streets.

Find someone to talk to who *does* understand. Your doctor. A neighbour. A friend. You should try to talk about your wife and your love. You have every right to miss her and it is perfectly understandable that you should feel the way you do. You should ignore those who thoughtlessly want you to 'meet new people'. Remember the good times you had together. Don't be ashamed to get out your photo album. Don't be afraid to cry. Enjoy, cherish and share your memories for it is your wife's love for you which will help you through the seemingly endless days of pain and loneliness. Your grief and sadness will never go completely but time will give you the strength to live with your sorrow.

....

SHOULD BE GRATEFUL

You and people like you should be grateful to live in Britain. Our society is free, people's individual rights are respected and everyone is free to express their opinion—however bizarre.

What joy to find such innocence and naivety. My phone is tapped so heavily that it constantly bleeps and plays back recordings of what I said last week. Private detectives follow me around in such numbers that I'm thinking of hiring a coach for them. And if my car inexplicably goes out of control and I end up squashed under a large lorry I hope someone will investigate the accident carefully.

··

THINGS GOT OUT OF HAND

During a recent holiday in Ilfracombe my husband and I were sitting cuddling on a bench overlooking the sea when things got rather out of hand. We both decided we wanted more than just a cuddle but our hotel was about two miles away and we didn't want to wait that long. We ended up making love on the bench with me sitting on his lap with my knickers in my handbag and my dress pulled up to my thighs. It was the best sex either of us have ever had. What made it exciting was that several people walked by as we were doing it and no one had any idea what we were up to. Afterwards we did it outdoors on several other occasions. Is there any law about having sex in public places? Could we get into trouble if we got caught?

I'm sure you could get into trouble if you got caught, for outdoor sex is bound to be a breach of some penal code. I haven't the foggiest idea what they'd do you for. Behaviour likely to lead to a breach of the peace? Behaviour likely to make puritanical presbyterians feel jealous and extremely upset? Behaviour likely to make other people realise what they've been missing for the past 96 years? Behaviour likely to result in a large crowd of people gathering and yelling bawdy encouragement? One thing is for sure: if you're spotted enjoying yourselves in public there is bound to be a law against it and the end result will be that having been screwed by your husband you'll get screwed by the system.

My carefully thought out advice is that you should try not to get caught. And if you do get spotted then have a good excuse ready. Alternatively, I know of one couple who escaped prosecution at a Northern seaside resort by arguing that they were both just trying to keep warm. With the right excuse you'd probably get a discharge—which is, I suppose, where your troubles started.

....

I NEED HELP

I got involved in a threesome recently and now I need some help. I met a couple in a disco who invited me back to their flat. When we got there the two of them started talking about sex. I was embarrassed but the woman started fondling me and her husband made it pretty clear that he didn't object to what was going on. Eventually the woman took me by the hand and led me into the bedroom. Her husband followed and got into bed with us. I made love to the woman and then her husband made love to her. While I was dozing the husband started fondling me. I was rather shocked and didn't say or do anything—even when he started making love to me I let him do what he wanted. I haven't told anyone else about what happened but now I'm very confused.

When you've visited your local Sexually Transmitted Diseases clinic to make sure that your sexual adventure hasn't left you with any physical souvenirs, you need to sit yourself down and think carefully about what happened.

What did you expect was going to happen when you went back to that flat? Are you really so naive that you thought that the three of you were going to talk about crop prices in the American Mid west and maybe play a little Monopoly for bottle tops? You must surely have expected some sort of sexual contact. If you now feel that what happened went way too far for you then you should be more careful in future about going home with strangers.

I suspect that you may also be confused about the homosexual element of your sexual adventure. Maybe you even enjoyed it and feel guilty about that. But remember that

one homosexual experience doesn't mean that you are gay
or even bisexual.

Since you are clearly sensitive and perhaps not ready for
a no-holds-barred sex life, you need to think carefully
about exactly what you want to do with your body.

A NEW DIET

I am just over a stone overweight. A friend has told me that
she lost her excess weight by masturbating several times
every day. She says that having lots of orgasms is a very
effective way of burning up calories. Is this so? If so then
this is a diet I think I could really enjoy.

You can get rid of about 150 calories by masturbating to
orgasm. You need to burn up 3,500 calories to lose a
pound of fat. So if you masturbate to orgasm 23 times that
will get rid of one pound. Since you need to lose a stone
you'll need to masturbate to orgasm 322 times to reach your
desired weight. And this assumes that your calorie intake
and other activities remain unaltered. I suggest you
produce a book and video about this new diet. You could
make a fortune. You could call it *Toss Off Those Unwanted
Pounds* or *Smile Your Way To Slenderness*.

MUMMY'S BOY

My husband is a real 'mummy's boy' and it's getting me
down. I thought he would change after we got married but
he hasn't. Even though she is perfectly fit and healthy and
has friendly neighbours he calls in to see her every evening
on the way home from work. Sometimes he has his tea
there and doesn't get back to me until nearly bedtime.
Every Sunday his mother comes round to our house and
stays for dinner and tea. Since I work on Saturdays this
means that my only day off is taken up with looking after
his mother, who is perfectly capable of looking after
herself. Once or twice I've suggested going out on a

Sunday but my husband always says that his mother would be disappointed if we broke the routine. In a funny sort of way I think he is frightened of her; she certainly has a hold over him.

Some mothers just can't get used to the idea of handing over their sons to other women. Many keep their sons on a tight rein by the careful use of guilt—the most deadly weapon ever invented. Throwing out loaded gems such as 'Don't you worry about me, I'll be all right. You go off and enjoy yourself' and 'Mrs Feynstropp's boy always calls in to see her every morning. Such a nice, thoughtful, loving son' makes son-control a psychological art form.

Tackling your son's mother head on could be a dangerous and bloody game. Instead I suggest that you try a little subtle manipulation of your own. What does your husband really love? Motor cars? Fell walking? Outdoor sex? Watersports? Stamp collecting? There must be something and when you've decided what it is start looking for Sunday events that you know he'll enjoy. Just hand him a newspaper cutting or brochure and let him make the first escape move himself.

Alternatively, you could try inviting your relatives or friends over on Sundays. Mother in law probably won't be too keen on having to share centre stage and a couple of noisy barbecues should do the trick.

....

MY PENIS IS SMALL

Are there are any exercises I can do or drugs I can take to make my penis bigger? My penis is quite small and I am very self conscious about it.

I know it isn't easy but do try not to be so concerned. 'No man and no church shall be judged by the size of their organs,' wrote Mrs Confucius, wife of the famous Chinese philosopher and bon vivant, and she certainly knew of what she spoke.

HELP ME

I have spent most of my life dieting. Every time I try a new diet it works well for a few months and then gradually I put back on every pound I've lost. I've decided that I am going to make one last effort. Can you please help me lose weight permanently?

The basic trick to losing weight permanently isn't just to change what you eat but to change when and why you eat. *What* you put into your mouth is far less important than *how much* and *how often*.

MY GIRLFRIEND PASSED OUT

While I was making love to my girlfriend recently she passed out. She came round again after half a minute and told me not to worry. She said it happened a lot to her. I've never come across this before, have you?

I have no personal experience of this phenomenon but it's known as the 'little death' and is quite common—particularly among women. Some individuals have a sort of semi fit. Others just drift into unconsciousness. It can be very scary for the partner who remains awake. Individuals who pass out regularly should warn new partners beforehand to avoid the embarrassment of coming to in an ambulance.

TEN LOVERS

A couple of weeks after we met my boyfriend asked me how many men I had been to bed with. I couldn't lie to him so I told him the truth: four. Since then it has been obvious that he doesn't trust or respect me. Every time we go out he accuses me of eyeing someone up. If I go out with friends he hits me and accuses me of sleeping with someone. Now we hardly ever go out and when we do I try not to speak to men. Whenever we argue about anything he throws it in my face. He hits me and says he'd never hit a woman, only a slag. No one could regret their past more than me. I would do anything to change it but I can't. It all happened when I was quite young and though it is no excuse I just lacked confidence and got in with the wrong crowd. I never made love before I met my boyfriend—men just used me for sex.

I want to forget about it but my boyfriend says he can never forgive me, that people never change and that I am cheap. He is always telling me that I am ugly and boring and that men are only interested in me for one thing. He says a lot of women fancy him and that he only stays with me because he feels sorry for me. He talks about making love with other women and tells me how much better other women are. Do you think I should just end the relationship as I only seem to be hurting my boyfriend. I realise that no man could ever love or respect me after what I did, so maybe I had better be on my own so that I can't hurt anyone and my boyfriend can have a chance of true love and happiness with a real woman. Please don't tell me that it's all my own fault. I know that. I just want to know what to do for the best.

Please try to stop feeling so guilty. Your sexual history is neither unusual nor any cause for shame. A recent survey showed that two thirds of all women have had at least six lovers while one in six women have had 25 or more lovers. Whatever has inspired your boyfriend's behaviour—jealousy for example—is no excuse. In my opinion no real man or genuine lover would be in the slightest bit concerned about your past sexual history.

If you care for him and want to make the relationship work then you should try to talk to your boyfriend and explain to him how hurtful you find his behaviour. If he can't or won't honestly accept that your past sexual adventures are now irrelevant then your relationship can have no future. But if you leave him remember that you are doing so for your sake and not for his. It is his behaviour which is unreasonable.

....

No erection

I tried to make love to my girlfriend recently but could not get an erection—even though I was very enthusiastic. I am very worried. Can you help me? Will this happen again?

There are many possible explanations. Most men suffer from impotence occasionally. I am reliably informed that it happens to male porn stars so often that blue movie directors have stunt organs on hand in case the intended star of the show doesn't stand up to close scrutiny at the most important moment. I suggest you see your doctor.

....

Irresponsible

My brother has sex with a different woman every week and boasts that he never uses a condom. How can I persuade him that this is irresponsible? I have only had sex with three different women in the last year and yet I always use a condom.

People do all sorts of daft things for all sorts of daft reasons. Just look at the number of people who drink and drive—or pay good money to jump out of aeroplanes. For heaven's sake, there are apparently still people who defy all logic and common sense and vote Conservative! You can tell your brother the facts and you can fill him up to the ears with good advice but you can't force him to behave sensibly.

....

My fat doctor

When I visited my doctor recently he told me that I needed to lose weight and that I should stop smoking. I couldn't help laughing about this when I got home. My doctor is even fatter than I am and smokes like a chimney.

Your doctor may not have the strength of mind to practise what he preaches but his advice is good. Now that you've enjoyed the joke I strongly suggest that you try to put his advice into practice. However, if your doctor ever offers you advice about how to improve your willpower I think you can safely ignore him.

....

UNSUCCESSFUL RELATIONSHIPS

I am female, in my early forties, live alone and run my own successful business. Since my divorce three years ago I have had several unsuccessful relationships. Two of the men I had affairs with just wanted me for money and another's hobby was punching—with me as the target. For a while I decided to give up men completely—on the grounds that they are more trouble than they are worth—but I missed sex terribly and found masturbation and vibrators a rather unsatisfactory alternative. Two months ago a girlfriend in a similar situation told me that she had been happily paying for sex for over a year. She gave me the telephone number of the escort agency she used and, after hesitating for several days, I eventually rang them and made my first 'date'. Although the young man from the agency was a real hunk I wasn't completely sure whether I'd take him to bed until we'd had dinner. He was good fun and made me laugh and clearly spent a lot of time in the gym so I did take him to bed and he was fantastic. It was a real joy to have a man whose sole aim was to give me pleasure. Even before he entered me I had had a string of breath-taking orgasms. I now ring the agency at least once a week and usually see a different man every time. The sex has always been great—the guys always bring plenty of condoms and use them (I'm very strict about practising 'safe sex') and they are never reluctant to perform oral sex (which I enjoy but have often found men unwilling to perform)! Occasionally I feel guilty about what I'm doing. What do you think?

Prostitution is the best established (and probably the most honest) of all professions and the use of male prostitutes by women is not a new development. Gigolos have been humping for money for centuries. I don't think you should feel in the slightest bit guilty about buying sexual favours when the alternatives are celibacy, masturbation or, as you sadly say, a series of unsatisfying relationships. For your sake I hope that do you find a man with whom you can have a complete, rounded relationship (including physical, mental and spiritual contact and comfort) because I suspect that you will then find the sex even more satisfying. But until then I can think of absolutely no moral reasons why you shouldn't carry on buying physical satisfaction.

TOO MUCH SEX?

Why do you write so much about sex?

Because people write to me with their sexual problems. And clearly want to read about sex. When most of the letters I get are about ingrowing toe nails then I'll devote more space to ingrowing toe nails.

MUSCLE TENSION

I am a 48-year-old male. I suffer from muscle tension in my shoulders and back. I know the tension develops because of my job. My doctor says there is nothing wrong with me and nothing he can do. What can you recommend?

Beg, borrow or hire a woman. For this treatment a woman with large breasts will be especially useful. Get her to take all her clothes off and kneel astride you. Then ask her to gently stroke every part of your body except your shoulders and back with her naked breasts. This mammary massage will not eradicate the tension from your shoulder muscles but it will cause tension in all the other muscles of your body and so you will be less aware of your problem.

. . . .

SHALL I GO ALL THE WAY?

My boyfriend wants me to make love to some of his friends and I don't know what to do. Every Saturday evening he and a group of four or five mates go out for a curry together. They usually come back to our flat afterwards. Two or three weeks ago my boyfriend insisted on showing a video he'd taken when we were on holiday in Spain. The video included several shots of me topless on the beach. The video went down very well and when my boyfriend suggested that I show off my boobs for real I did. I didn't want to at first but I'd had quite a lot to drink and they were all egging me on. Now my boyfriend wants me to let his mates all have sex with me. I really don't want to but my boyfriend says that after I bared my boobs his pals are expecting me to go all the way with them.

Tell your boyfriend that you think that exposing your breasts was a mistake. Then arrange to spend the next few weekends with your mother/sister/best friend/aunt in Cleethorpes/Sunderland/Bristol/Dover.

If your boyfriend still tries to insist that you have sex with his chums I suggest that you trade him in for something more sensitive. This won't be difficult. A vibrator would be more sensitive.

. . . .

ELDERLY AND BAD TEMPERED

My parents are both elderly and extremely bad tempered. Neither I, my husband nor any of my children can ever do anything right.

Irascibility and irritability are as much a part of old age as wrinkles, liver spots and thinning hair. Years of frustration and world weariness are probably the primary cause, though physical infirmities and a sad realisation that life really is a bitch are probably contributory factors. There is no treatment for the age related irritability. Elderly relatives who enjoy poor health are like nymphomaniacs in short, tight skirts. Both are difficult to satisfy— and impossible to get into and out of motor cars.

NO ONE I CAN TRUST

I am very lonely. I don't have any real friends and there is no one I can really trust.

Try talking—and listening—to animals. You should be able to obtain peace, comfort and good advice. Animals are honest, straightforward and, if unthreatened, generally full of love. These are not qualities which are widely available among members of the biped master species.

NO PURPOSE

My life doesn't seem to have any real purpose. I get up, go to work, watch TV, go to bed and then do it all again. More and more often I've found myself asking what it's all for.

Set aside a little time for thinking about what you are doing with your life. What do you want out of whatever years you have left? What are your passions? What are you committed to? What drives you? What do you really want to do with your life: change the world, have fun or make money? Once you understand what you want from your life then you will be in a better position to make sure that you go some way towards getting it. One tip: *time* is the most important, most fundamental currency in the world: the only currency that really matters. Unless you are one of the lucky few who really enjoy what you do—and would do it even if you didn't get paid for it—then when you go to work you sell your time for money. And you must then use that money to pay for the quality time in your life. Try to relate the amount you need to earn to what you want to do with your income and try to balance the time you spend earning it against the time that remains for pleasure.

....

I ENJOY WEARING SKIRTS

I am a middle aged man who enjoys wearing skirts. I am a bit bored with just wearing them around the house. I want to go out wearing a skirt. Do you think it would be more acceptable to other people if I put on a wig and make up and tried to look like a woman? I don't want to be a woman and I'm not a pervert: I just like wearing feminine clothes. My wife says I should put on a skirt and go out as myself. I would prefer to do this.

If you lived in some other countries (or had been born in a different century) you would be able to go out dressed in a skirt without anyone raising an eyebrow. But I fear that you will be asking for trouble if you try it in this country today. In our guilt laden society there is a real danger that you will be sneered at by the repressed, laughed at by the prejudiced, beaten up by the ignorant and then arrested for causing a breach of the peace. If you want to go out of the house wearing visible feminine clothing you will, I'm afraid, have to do the job properly. The more convincingly you can make yourself look like a woman, the smaller the risk of any sort of confrontation.

....

MY WIFE IS RATHER PLAIN

I am bright and good looking but my wife is rather plain. I deliberately married her because I wanted an obedient wife and felt that an ordinary looking woman would make a better wife than a woman who knew that she was pretty. We have been married for nearly 15 years and I've been very good to her. I have always taken her with me to the golf club and let her sit in the car while I play. On many occasions I have taken her into the club-house with me so that she can have a drink. I have always been very good to her and have dutifully made love to her every Saturday night even though I have obtained little pleasure from this myself. Recently I have noticed a change in her. She hasn't been argumentative or troublesome in any obvious way but she has joined a writing circle (although I would not have thought she was bright enough for that sort of thing) and I was shocked this week to discover that she has been taking painting lessons and has joined an aerobics class. She has begun to ignore me and to offer comments of her own when I have been entertaining visitors. I have been a very good husband and I think she has been very lucky to be my wife. Why do you think she is behaving like this? Her whole outlook on life has changed.

I checked the postmark on the envelope in which your letter arrived and was surprised to see that your query was, indeed, posted this century. I can only assume that you must be living in one of those funny little villages where folk are busy bricking up their windows to avoid the 'window tax' and where individual freedom and emancipation are still regarded as rather frightening and alien concepts. If, as I suspect, you have one of those bolt on heads that can be easily detached then I suggest that you order one of your serfs to remove the whole area north of your neck, place it in a cauldron and boil it for several hours over a log fire. After this treatment your head can be replaced and rebolted and you may find that you are able to think a little more clearly.

··

THE THREE OF US

My boyfriend and his cousin are really close and the three of us spend a lot of time together. One night recently, after an evening at the pub, my boyfriend suggested that his cousin should stay the night with us—in our bed—instead of catching the bus home. He made it pretty clear that they were both going to have sex with me. I was shocked and said 'no'. Since then I've thought about it and have regretted that I refused. My boyfriend hasn't mentioned the idea since but I can't get the thought out of my head. I'm sure my boyfriend would still be keen. And I know his cousin fancies me. Do you think I would be making a mistake if I suggested it?

There's a lot of difference between an exciting sexual fantasy and the sometimes messy, often confusing and invariably 'loaded' consequence of turning that fantasy into reality. I suggest you beware and think carefully. Sharing your body with your boyfriend and his cousin will dramatically change your relationship with your boyfriend, his relationship with his cousin, your relationship with his cousin and his cousin's relationship with you. None of these relationships will ever be the same again. They may be better and they may be worse. But they won't be the same. Not even the cactus on the bathroom shelf will look at you in quite the same way. If you *want* to change your whole life then maybe a night of fantasy sex will produce dramatic results which you welcome. But if you're happy with things as they are, the price you have to pay for a few hours of sexual adventure could be a high one.

· ·

ANGRY AND UPSET

What makes you most angry and upset?

Every week I get armfuls of letters from people who have had a raw deal and who need help. I can't help them and that makes me angry and upset. Sadly, there just aren't enough hours in the day. I am angered, saddened to tears and frustrated by injustice and cruelty; both of which are endemic in our society. One of the great ironies (and in turn one of the great injustices) of life is that I get the feeling from my mailbag that those who are responsible for the worst cruelties and injustices with which our world is tainted rarely seem to suffer guilt or anguish as a result of their actions. It is, it seems to me, the innocent and sensitive, frustrated by their inability to stop these outrages, who are tortured by the knowledge of those deeds and who seem to do all the suffering on behalf of the perpetrators.

NASTY RUMOURS

People I work with have recently been spreading nasty rumours about me. The rumours are not true but they are very hurtful. Several people who I thought were friends will no longer talk to me.

Look on the bright side: at least you now know the identities of those individuals who you thought were friends but who weren't really friends at all! I know it is difficult to do so but try to rise above the rumours by ignoring them. Once you start trying to counter lies you will find your life taken over by justifiable anger and a constant sense of frustration. Try to comfort yourself with the knowledge that in the end it doesn't matter what people say about you unless you or those who are really close to you (and whose love and support is important to you) believe them.

WORK AT HOME

Six months ago I started to work at home. I still do the same job as before but my employer has equipped me with a computer so that can I work in a bedroom instead of travelling every day. At first it seemed ideal but now I'm having second thoughts about it. I find the life very lonely and seem to get depressed far more often than before. Is it possible for working at home to affect me this way?

Yes. It's now well accepted that working at home isn't always emotionally healthy. People need to talk to others. By isolating ourselves with electronic equipment we deny ourselves human contact. In America people who work at home are known as 'hermies'—slang for hermits—and there is a real danger that things could get worse for you if you don't do something soon. My advice: make sure you get out of the house several times a week. Join local clubs, groups or associations so that you have fixed commitments which mean that you leave home regularly.

SACKED

One of the women I work with has been sacked because she has cancer and needs to take time off occasionally for hospital appointments. We have complained but been told that it has nothing to do with us.

Keep complaining. Transportation to Australia has been stopped and the worst they can do is sack you all. And do you really want to work for people who don't feel that there is anything wrong in sacking a woman because she has cancer?

MY BEST FRIEND AND I

When my husband started a new job he had to go on a course. It meant that he couldn't take me to a dinner and dance for which he had already booked tickets. My husband suggested that rather than waste the tickets I should take my best friend with me. Shortly after we arrived two attractive men started chatting us up. By the end of the evening neither of us was capable of driving. The two men said that they had a bedroom booked for each of them and that my friend and I could have one room and stay the night. But it soon became obvious that my friend was going to sleep with the man she'd been dancing with. The man I'd spent the evening with said I could share his bed and promised me that he wouldn't touch me. We did both try to sleep apart but eventually the inevitable happened and we ended up making love. It was wonderful. The next morning the bloke I'd spent the night with gave me his phone number and told me he'd like to see me again. Now I don't know what to do. Since my husband started this new job he has been unbearable. He is constantly irritable and always too tired for sex. I know I should be more understanding but I can't stop thinking about my wonderful night of love. My husband spends several nights a week away from home and I am very tempted to ring and arrange another evening out with the man I met at the dinner and dance—but I don't know whether or not I should.

You're asking yourself the wrong question. Instead of asking yourself whether or not you should be unfaithful again—and, presumably, start a rip roaring, guilt laden affair—you should be asking yourself whether or not you want your marriage to succeed.

If you do regard your relationship with your husband as important then you should be working hard to rescue a marriage which seems to be teetering on the brink of failure.

If you think your marriage is over then the question which follows is: 'Am I going to get divorced, or am I going to plod on and get my kicks out of one or more affairs?'

The really big question which you have to answer is: 'Do I love my husband?' Answer that one and all the other questions will more or less answer themselves.

....

THE MEDICINE MEN

I've just seen a programme on TV about women who developed cancer because their mothers took a drug during pregnancy. Is it possible that any other drugs could have this sort of effect?

I haven't got the foggiest idea. And I don't believe anyone else knows either. I first exposed this hazard (and warned about the cancer link you saw described on TV) in a book called *The Medicine Men* which was published in 1975. At the time there had not been any cases identified in the UK. I was, inevitably, dismissed by the establishment as a lunatic. My only practical suggestion is that all pregnant women should do their best to avoid taking unnecessary drugs (and that includes medication bought directly from the chemist and alternative remedies). If you are pregnant and your doctor prescribes a drug for you, ask him if you really need it and if the risk is worthwhile.

....

TREATED LIKE A CHILD

I'm in my early twenties and have two problems with my parents. First, they still treat me like a child. I think they believe that being old means that they know everything. I have a responsible job and a nice flat but they still nag me about my clothes and my hair. Second, they are often unbelievably rude to my friends. I've noticed that many old people are amazingly rude. They say things that they would never accept from someone my age.

At the age of 19 we all go through a phase of life known as the 'tact barrier'. We wake up one morning and realise that if we wrap up our prejudices a little, and think before we speak, we will get on better with people. We acquire a 'tact veneer'. As the years go by this socially essential 'tact veneer' becomes weak, wrinkly and cracked and prejudices peep through the gaps. At the same time there is often a paradoxical hypersensitisation to criticism. This is why old people become so rude and then get really miffed if you dare to say anything to them. There is no treatment. The only answer is to keep out of their way as much as possible when the 'tact veneer' cracks become really noticeable.

Fortunately, there are symptoms to show when old folk are starting to lose their 'tact veneer'. They will dress almost exclusively in beige, become unbelievably self centred and selfish and talk only about their feet and their bowels. Females suffering from 'tact deprivation' carry folding umbrellas and huge, sensible, imitation plastic shopping bags crammed with spare jumpers, thermos flasks and knitting patterns. Males wear sandals and a haunted look and spend most of their time making sure that they aren't more than 100 yards from a public lavatory. 'Tact deprived' old people often live on coaches and eat in restaurants which triple cook all food so that it is suitable for the artificially dentured.

. . . .

BRA, SUSPENDER BELT AND STOCKINGS

My husband often dresses up in women's clothes. He frequently comes to bed wearing a bra, suspender belt and stockings. I'm surprised to have to admit that I find this a real turn on. Is this something I should worry about?

Many women who are married to (or live with) trans-vestites or cross dressers are sexually excited by making love to their partners when they are 'dressed'. Any psychoanalyst could spend years investigating the reasons behind this phenomenon—and probably send his kids to private school on the proceeds. My advice is that you completely ignore the underlying reasons, suppress your anxieties, buy your husband more sexy underwear and just enjoy yourself.

. . . .

MISSING OUT

I've been married for eight years and I can't remember when we last had sex. I think we probably do it about half a dozen times a year. I don't really mind—we have a good relationship in other ways—but I sometimes think I'm missing out on something. My best friend, who has been married about the same length of time as I have, says that she and her husband do it two or three times a week.

People lie most about two things: money and sex. They usually claim that they are getting more of both than they really are. (Oddly, the third and fourth on the list of things people commonly lie about are how much tobacco they smoke and how much alcohol they drink. In each case people over 21 invariably minimise their consumption of these goodies. Teenagers lie in the opposite direction; but then that's hardly surprising because they don't count as real people.)

It is a myth that most people have sex two or three times a week and the chances are that your friend is telling whopping pork pies. In most relationships time has a deadening effect on sexual urges. Familiarity tends to breed contentment. A wise old man in Dorking once said that if a young couple put a penny into a jar every time they have sex for the first six months of their marriage, and then take out a penny every time they have sex after the first six months, they will never empty the jar.

If you're genuinely content then take no notice of your friend's boasts. If, on the other hand, you fancy more nookie than you're getting then try adding a little spice to your marriage. Buy yourself some sexy lingerie and forget to put a frock on next time you're serving up hubby's meal.

....

WITHOUT QUALIFICATIONS

I left school without any qualifications and I've always had boring and poorly paid jobs. My husband works in a factory and although he works hard he doesn't earn much money either. About eighteen months ago I applied for, and got, a much better paid job—as a supervisor in a Bingo Hall. I've worked hard and two weeks ago I was told that if I wanted it I could have the job as Manager when the current Manager retires. At my age I'm not going to get many more chances like this. I'm really excited and proud of the progress I've made but my husband seems determined to spoil everything. He tells me that I'm getting above myself and accuses me of having an affair because I sometimes have to work late. He constantly puts a dampener on things. Things have got so bad that I don't like to talk to him about my work any more. I don't want to leave him but if it comes to choosing between him and the chance of a real job I may well choose the job.

Sit your husband down, turn off the TV and tell him what this job really means to you. If he can't or won't understand how you feel, you will be entirely justified in trading him in for a couple of toyboys—and then you'll be the one yelling 'Bingo!' every night.

• •

CONVENIENT

My boyfriend still sleeps with his ex-wife every Saturday night. He goes there to see his children and stays over because it's a long drive back. He insists that he doesn't love his ex-wife but sleeps with her because it's convenient. He says the sex with her doesn't mean anything and isn't a threat to our relationship.

The sex with her means something and is clearly a threat to your relationship. He's parking his pride and joy in the wrong garage and you need to repossess it. Point out to him that his regular infidelities are making you unhappy and either ask him to come home on Saturday nights or tell him that you'll go with him so that you can stay in a hotel together.

• •

NOT MY FAULT

I am five feet four inches tall and weigh thirteen and a half stones. What people don't understand is that there is a genetic reason for my excess weight. Both my father and mother were overweight. How can I make people realise that although I have a weight problem it is not my fault?

I hate to be a spoilsport but I'm afraid the chances are that you're kidding yourself. The chances are that you, your mother and your father are all fat because you eat too much. You are roughly 4 stones overweight. Each pound of unwanted fat is a result of an unnecessary 3,500 calories. So that means that you've consumed 196,000 calories that your body didn't need. That's the approximate equivalent of 600 doughnuts too many.

Your obesity is not just making it difficult for you to wear a bikini without looking like a 3D map of the butter mountain but it is also hazarding your health.

GIGGLING IN THE SHOWERS

What do women talk about in the showers? My girlfriend won't tell me but I can always hear her and the other girls giggling when they're changing.

I am reliably informed by those who know that all women in groups talk incessantly and almost exclusively about sex. Your girlfriend and her chums will be talking (and laughing) about the size, colour and shape of your penis, how often you do it, what sexual fetishes you have, how long you can last and so on. Next time you meet her out of the showers tell her that you overheard the conversation she and the other girls were having—and watch her go red!

REALLY DULL

My husband is really dull. When we were first married he was great fun. These days he is no fun at all. He seems to have grown very old. What can I do to liven him up a bit?

Most people get more boring and critical as they get older. When a kid sees a pile of leaves on the pavement he will run through them. Twenty years later that same kid will carefully walk round the pile of leaves. And thirty years afterwards the grown old version of that same kid will complain about the weather, write a letter of complaint to the local council about the danger of wet leaves on the pavements and recommend that all trees be chopped down and be replaced with better public lighting.

Your husband has undoubtedly got old because he has been weighed down and made weary by responsibility. Lighten his load in as many ways as you can and you may see some sparks of life in the old corpse.

CONSTANTLY EXHAUSTED

I do as you say and try to fight against injustice but I find that it makes me feel constantly exhausted.

Learn to pace yourself and to fight only those battles which you consider to be important. A few years ago a friend of mine and I once decided that we were going to fight every example of injustice we came across for a whole year. We decided that we would complain about everything we bought—even lightbulbs—that promptly went phut the moment they were asked to do what they were made to do. After six months we both gave up exhausted. Complaining and protesting had taken over our lives.

You have to be selective. Step away from the unimportant battles and keep your energy for the big battles that really matter. By all means make your feelings clear when you feel that you have come across a minor injustice but then walk away.

NO HOLIDAYS

My husband won't take time off work. He won't take holidays. He just works all the time. We don't have any money worries so I don't understand why he drives himself so hard. I am terrified that he's going to have a heart attack.

Workaholics usually push themselves because they lack self confidence. They constantly search for love and try to make themselves indispensible. By working hard they also get the entirely spurious feeling that they are in control. The truth is that workaholics lose love *and* lose control. Try to encourage your husband to find hobbies that he can become passionate about. And don't ever allow a day to go by without telling him how much you love him. Finally, reassure him frequently that you'll love him whether or not you have any money and try to convince him that it won't worry you whether you spend your lives in luxury or poverty.

....

MY BRUISE

While my girlfriend and I were making love I got into a rather tricky position and fell out of bed and banged my head. I had quite a big bruise as a result. Two days later I met three of the girls my girlfriend does aerobics with in a shop in town. One of the girls made a great show of examining my bruise and then told me that in future I should stick to the missionary position. All three of them then laughed and it was clear that my girlfriend had told them exactly what had happened. I was very surprised and embarrassed because I had never realised that women discussed things like sex when talking to one another. I had certainly never guessed that my girlfriend would talk about something so intimate to her friends.

Brace yourself. Even though they may never have seen you naked, your girlfriend's pals could probably identify your penis in the dark. They could probably all draw accurate maps of the veins which stand out when you're excited. And I'll give you long odds that they know all about that time you got drunk and tried on your girlfriend's stockings and suspender belt. I realise that it is sexist and politically incorrect to suggest that there are differences between the sexes but this is one area where the difference is oceanic in size. Male conversation tends to be confined to solid, straightforward, tangible subjects. Men talk about cars, plumbing and football. Female conversation is usually dominated by intimate details of emotional and physical relationships. Your girlfriend is no different to any other woman.

....

CORRUPTION AND DISHONESTY

I sometimes feel depressed when I look around and realise how many terrible things go on in this world. Everywhere you look there seems to be corruption and dishonesty. Ordinary people are constantly being shafted by politicians and businessmen. Do you think there is really any hope for any of us?

The battalions of evil are ranged far and wide, high and ugly. They stand firm against the weak and the poor. The meek won't inherit the earth because they have been disenfranchised. But live your life honestly and with good intentions and you will enjoy the comfort of a clear conscience; now probably the only quality asset in a harsh, cruel world.

....

A REAL HEEL

My husband was a real heel. He had a never ending string of girlfriends. He drank too much. He spent all our money and didn't have a sensible bone in his body. Last year I finally decided that I had had enough and threw him out. I haven't heard from him or seen him for months but I now realise that I miss him terribly. Do you think I should try and get in touch and ask him to come back to me?

Before you do anything you must answer a very simple question—and you must answer it honestly. Do you miss your husband because you love him or do you miss him because you are lonely? If you miss him because you love him, then by all means get in touch and find out whether or not he wants to come back to you. (But, before you do that, just try to remember exactly why you threw him out the first time.) If you miss him because you are lonely, then you would probably be better off acquiring a more reliable partner. I understand that terrapins make congenial companions.

....

THE STRIPPER

I hired a stripper for my husband's 40th birthday. I thought it would be a good joke. The girl was in her twenties and had a stupendous figure. My husband can't stop talking about the damned girl and has a photograph she gave him on his desk at work. I'm beginning to think that I made a serious mistake.

The age of 40 is something of a landmark. Consciously or subconsciously your husband is now facing up to the fact that for him the summer is nearly over and the early days of autumn are just a curling leaf away. His mild obsession with the stripper you hired for him is merely a symptom of a deeper malaise. He is having to come to terms with the fact that his wild days are over and his life is set into a pattern. These are dangerous days. It is the shock produced by coming to face with the shadow of the man with the scythe which explains why so many men who have just celebrated their 40th birthday suddenly abandon everything—wife, family, home and job—and run off with top heavy, gravity defying 18-year-old hairdressers.

You can help him by doing everything you can to reassure him that he is still young, virile and dangerous. Seduce him with candlelit dinners and sexy new clothes. Tell him how much you love him. (Men need to be told that they are loved every bit as much as women.) Encourage him to take up new hobbies and interests. And getting him to talk about his plans for the future will remind him that there *is* a future and that his life is not quite so nearly over as he might suspect.

BONDING

My husband goes out drinking with his mates at least three times a week. When I protested and told him I was fed up of being left by myself he told me that going out with other men was important to him because it kept him in touch with his maleness and helped him to gain strength by bonding with members of his own sex.

This nonsense about male bonding is, I suspect, popular with men who are fed up with doing the washing up and want a sound excuse for enjoying regular drinking and poker sessions with the boys. Buy your husband a good, old fashioned dirty magazine and make sure he doesn't come into contact with any more of those strange self improvement books.

OUTSPOKEN

I am very outspoken and often get into trouble at work. My husband says that I get too agitated about things and that I should try to be more objective. I find it difficult to see both sides of an argument. My husband says that if I don't change my ways I will lose my job. What do you think?

I think your husband is probably right. If you carry on the way you are there is a decent chance that you will, before long, find yourself discovering the joys of being allowed time to explore other employment possibilities. I regard this as sad but it is life and there is no point in denying it.

UNIMAGINATIVE

My husband is very unimaginative in bed. We make love quite often but it's always the same. He gets into bed, gropes my breasts for about a minute and a half (that's his idea of foreplay) and then climbs on top of me and pumps away as though he's in the gym. Sex lasts for between two and five minutes (I know because I get so bored that I've found myself timing him). When he's finished he uses his fingers to give me an orgasm and then he turns over and falls asleep. I'd like to do it a different way once in a while. Just once I'd like him to undress me and make love to me while I'm still wearing my underwear. I would desperately like to make love in front of the fire. I'd like to try oral sex (which I have never, ever done with anyone). How do I persuade my husband to add a little excitement to our sex life? I did once try playing with him while he was fondling my breasts but I think he was rather shocked by this.

Why do you have to persuade him to change your love making ritual? Sex is not something he does to you; it is something you share. Take charge yourself. Whisper the details of your favourite fantasies into his ear the next time his hand reaches out for your breast. Shyly tell him what you'd like him to do to you. You can lead each other into a new world of sexual excitement.

GET RICH QUICK

I don't really like work very much but I would very much like to make a lot of money. I've spent months looking for a way to get rich quick without any success. Have you any suggestions?

If you define 'work' as something that you don't enjoy doing, then the only way to make money without working is to find something you can make money out of that you *do* enjoy doing! The added advantage will be that if you spend your days doing something you enjoy, then you will inevitably work harder and better than if you spend your days doing something you hate. One of the odd truths about our society is that a few people become extremely rich without ever really working while most people work hard all their lives and never make any real money.

FLATTERED

I am a keen member of my local dramatic society. We've just finished a production of a farce in which I had to run around on stage in my underwear. I've got a very good figure (by that I mean that I've got big breasts) and to be honest I rather enjoyed my part. I got quite a kick out of knowing that all the men in the audience were watching my every move. I've now been approached by a man who wants me to act in a movie he is making. He has been very honest with me and told me that he wants me to take all my clothes off in several scenes. He says he will pay me for my work and isn't worried by the fact that I don't have an Equity card. My husband says he doesn't mind if the nudity is essential. I am very flattered by the prospect of being in a film but just a little bit wary. Do you think I am right to be cautious or should I just go ahead and make the film?

If you want to know exactly what you're letting yourself in for, then insist that the movie maker lets you see some of his other work and ask to see a copy of the shooting script. Find out who will be sharing your scenes. And what you and they will be doing together. I have a suspicion that you're more likely to find your bottom and breasts taking starring roles than you are to find your thespian skills being tested to the limits. I bet you a laddered stocking to a St Laurent original that you've been invited to make a blue movie and you're more likely to be playing Jane the Big Boobed Randy Typist than Ophelia, the fey heroine. If you (and your husband) are happy with that, then that's fine. But find out now what sort of film stardom you are being offered.

RESERVATIONS

I love my boyfriend very much and plan to marry him early next year. But I do have some reservations and anxieties. My boyfriend is rather short tempered and can be quite moody if things aren't going right for him. He can be quick to take offence and often tends to act first and think later. He is very talented but I wonder whether or not I might find his faults difficult to live with.

Only you can decide whether your love for your boyfriend is great enough to counterbalance his faults. But do remember that any man without vices would be dull indeed. Faults are just as much an essential part of any individual character as are virtues. Your boyfriend might be a more admirable character if he was more guarded, less quick to take offence and less likely to act spontaneously. But the zest, the 'punch', the vitality, the piquancy and the talent you admire are a result of a combination of vices and virtues. Remove the vices and you would be left with a very different human being.

....

GRKEHL DKENKW

What can you tell me about dyslexia?

Hjkley nimokl qwert yuiop, ludiope nvcemni ar bkj pioyl triolx caruncle etiopi! Brawtyle zalipop nam yimjle cim xod. Proxle grutip nimtradfeltinger bram digdpe rintwep cxudyj fghjk peynkel. Ho gtyrle bridme qwon.

....

BREAKING THE LAW

I work for a company which is, I know, breaking the law by polluting a local river. Should I say anything? Would it be disloyal to 'blow the whistle' on my company?

You have to decide where your primary loyalties lie—to the company which pays your wages or to the community in which you live. And you must remember that those who tolerate evil are touched and contaminated by the evil they tolerate. Those who are silent in the face of wrongdoing are as guilty as those who do wrong.

AN HONOUR

I have received a letter telling me that I am being considered for an honour by my old college. But there are my things about the college which I no longer approve of and although I'm flattered by the honour I don't feel entirely comfortable about accepting it. I have, indeed, been a fairly vocal critic of some of the college's policies. What do you think I should do?

You should turn down the honour and explain exactly why you are turning it down. If you accept an honour then you are publicly allying yourself with the institution which is awarding you the honour. And how can you criticise the college in future if you have accepted an honour? Anyone who accepts an honour from an organisation is adding whatever credence, credibility and prestige they may have to the organisation concerned. Governments, monarchs and institutions constantly seek to win favour, support (and, sometimes, silence) by handing out awards and honours.

TREATED AS EQUALS

I work in an office with several women. We get on quite well together. I make sure that I always treat them as equals. For example, I always take my turn at making the coffee (whereas in another nearby office it is always the two women who make the coffee). My problem is that the women I work with are sexist in the way they regard me. For example, they always expect me to do any heavy lifting or other physical work that needs doing around the office. I suffer with back trouble and two of the women are bigger and probably stronger than I am!

The dilemma you describe is one of the commonest men face. If a man stands up on a train to give a woman his seat then he is likely to be branded a sexist pig. If he doesn't stand up then he's a rude bastard. It is this no-win stress producing conflict which helps explain why most men die several years earlier than most women. Next time you think you are being treated differently because of your sex try pointing out to your colleagues what they are doing. Women are often unaware that they are behaving in a sexist way.

....

SEVEN YEARS LONGER

Why do women live longer than men?

In recent years women have quite reasonably claimed the right to do nearly all of the things that men do—and to behave in many traditionally male ways.

(There are, of course, a few exceptions—the most notable being the almost universal failure of women to master the art of peeing while standing up with their legs together.)

Women now fight fires, drive lorries and sit in the boss's chair and exhibit emotions which were traditionally regarded as male—and which, in the past, women have usually had to suppress. But while women have won the right to spit, swear and arm wrestle—without losing their feminine qualities—most men still don't feel able to exhibit traditionally female qualities.

The truth is that at heart most men are just as romantic, compassionate and sensitive as most women. But most men dare not admit their femininity to themselves—let alone show it to others. As a result men are suffering genuine physical harm.

A few decades ago men and women had the same sort of life expectancy. Today's figures show that women now live seven years longer than men. And men now die earlier than women from all 15 leading causes of death—including heart disease, cancer and suicide. Nursing homes throughout the country are now full of lonely old women who have outlived their male partners. There is no biological explanation for this. Women are not intrinsically healthier than men. The explanation has to be found in the way that women have changed their role in society. And there is a vital lesson here for all men—and for all women who love men.

Men should not be ashamed to show their female qualities; they should not be reluctant to let their emotions show, to ask for help and support and to combine traditional male toughness with the soft, gentle qualities which are hidden deep inside. And women should do their best to encourage their men to show their femininity. These days it isn't women who need liberating but men.

Here are five practical ways in which men can let their soft, feminine nature surface:

1. Don't hide your fears and vulnerability.
2. Learn to listen to your instincts more often.
3. Share your feelings with friends.
4. Show your hurt—rather than burying it.
5. Don't be afraid to let people see your compassionate side.

THE PROSTITUTE

My husband regularly visits a prostitute who lives near to us. He spends so much on her that there is not enough left for us to pay rent or housekeeping and although we both have jobs I constantly have to borrow money off my mother and my sister. I have repeatedly asked my husband to stop seeing this woman but he refuses. He says she satisfies him much better than I do in bed. I feel guilty about my inability to make him happy but it hurts me to know that he is with her so often and the shortage of money is making my life unbearable. I get very fed up when I think of him lying in bed with her and then paying her with money I have earned.

Your husband is thoughtless, selfish, unprincipled and contemptible. Leave him. Pack up your belongings and abandon him. He is an evil cad, a foul breathed bounder, an unforgivable blackguard with no redeeming features and a miscreant with the grace of silage. Your life will be brighter, your future rosier and your world more joyful if you wipe the memory of this dark hearted slubber-degullion from your spirit for ever.

··

SIMPLE TASTES

My girlfriend and I both have very simple tastes. We live in a fairly small house, drive a cheap car and don't have many possessions. We work together at home and although we could work longer hours we are content to make less money and have more time to spend on the things we enjoy doing. My parents are very critical and constantly encourage us to work harder in order 'to improve our situation'. But we're quite happy the way we are.

Stay as you are. It is a virtue and a strength to have simple tastes. You will live healthier, happier (and probably longer) lives if you stand firm together against your parents' attempt to drag you into the horrors of the acquisitive society.

··

SECOND CLASS

I work in education. I'm white and male and I'm beginning to feel like a second class citizen. I've applied for promotion on several occasions. Each time I've been told that my qualifications are perfect and my work record exemplary. But each time the job has been given to someone else. On four occasions the 'someone else' has been female, black and had fewer qualificiations and less experience than I have. I'm beginning to feel that I have no chance of ever getting anywhere. I have always been fervently opposed to racism but it seems to me that I am now suffering from racist policies.

The process you describe is well established in South Africa where it is known as 'affirmative action'. The excuse is that since blacks have been discriminated against for years there now needs to be some discrimination against whites in order to redress the balance. I think 'affirmative action' is dangerous for it will eventually lead to a backlash. How much longer before hordes of middle aged white males troop onto the streets and start storming the citadels from whence these dangerous ideas are disseminated?

Meanwhile, the process you describe has spread far and wide. One white male author I know sent a book typescript to several publishers. None of them were interested. A few months later he persuaded a black woman friend to send the same typescript to the same publishers. Several of them were wildly enthusiastic and made offers for the book. The moral seems clear enough. In future I will be writing under another name and this column will be called Dr Blodwyn Ngwanda's Casebook.

....

INSURANCE CLAIM

I recently needed to claim on my insurance. The whole process nearly sent me potty. Every time I wrote a letter to one department I got a letter back from another department. And every letter needed new information and another form filling in. In the end I gave up. The claim was taking over my life. And no one would take any responsibility for what was happening. It isn't just insurance companies which play this game. Government departments are just as bad. No one seems to care any more.

Insurance companies use the wearing down process you describe to avoid paying out on claims. And government departments, which derive their power from individuals, seem to despise and heartily disapprove of individuals. It is the separation of responsibility from authority which is the most dangerous aspect of all modern bureaucracies. It is rare these days to find any employed individual who will accept responsibility. Even those who enjoy considerable authority fearlessly announce that they cannot possibly be expected to take any responsibility for what they do. The separation of responsibility from authority has undoubtedly been a major cause of stress in our society. The bureaucrats have created a deep black nightmare for us all to live in. The only faint ray of joy comes from the fact that they have to live in the same world and, in their turn, suffer the same frustrations that we have to put up with.

FOOD ADDITIVES

Do you think that chemical additives in food can be bad for you? I prefer to buy fresh food whenever possible but my mother claims that additives help to keep food longer. She points out that food that doesn't contain preservatives and other chemicals is more likely to go 'bad'.

I think that eating fresh food (preferably grown organically) is much healthier than eating food which is impregnated with chemicals. But if you eat fresh food then you must eat it while it is still fresh!

The presence of so many chemicals in food worries me. Many chemicals cause unpleasant, adverse reactions and I have no doubt at all that thousands of patients acquire allergies to chemicals in food. I also worry about the hidden effect of chemicals. Homoeopaths claim that putting very small amounts of a substance into water turns the water into a medicine. The whole principle of homoeopathy is based upon the fact that very small amounts of a chemical can have a dramatic effect on the human body. If homoeopathy works then the chemicals in our drinking water (which are there in much greater than homoeopathic doses) and the chemicals in our food must be having a horrifying effect on our health.

CHECK UP

I can't afford to have annual health check ups. But I do acknowledge the importance of preventive medicine. Have you any advice?

Learn to listen to your body. Study it daily as though you were looking at a stranger. Try to be observant, caring and critical. If you spot problems early you will be able to prevent small troubles becoming big worries. And learn to be aware of your body. So, for example, if you notice an ache in your back after sitting at your desk for an hour or two then change your position regularly.

LIFE EXPECTANCY

Doesn't the fact that life expectancy has improved enormously show the value of modern medicine?

It is a myth that we are all living much longer than our ancestors. Improved infant mortality rates have made it seem as though we are living longer but if you look back through the history books you'll find plenty of examples of men and women living well beyond their seventies. For example, when Henry David Thoreau's father died in 1859 he was described as having not been very old. He was 71. Back when the Bible was written a normal life expectation was 'three score years and ten'. The improvements which have taken place are largely a result of improvements in hygiene, sanitation, food supplies and living conditions which took place during the nineteenth century.

A NURSE WRITES

I am a hospital nurse. You are wrong to condemn vivisection. Animal experiments are essential if scientists are to find cures for cancer, AIDS and other diseases.

According to a piece of unpublished, illiterate research done by the heavily sedated 97-year-old Professor Josef Weissmantle of the Mengele Memorial Social Engineering Department at the downtown University of Barnstaple, you are right. According to 3,847,184,027,185,290 highly qualified doctors and scientists you are a dangerous, out of date lunatic. I commonly favour a contrarian view on social and scientific matters (on the grounds that the majority is usually misinformed, prejudiced and incapable of coherent thought) but in this instance I'm happy to be going with the flow. I suggest that you ask your colleagues to give you a brain scan. I suspect that you may be a Friday person— produced by God when he was looking forward to the weekend. The chances are that the scan will reveal that you have got your brain in upside down and need urgent remedial surgery. Meanwhile, I have arranged for the hospital where you work to keep you on permanent bed pan duty on the diarrhoea ward.

....

ENTIRELY VOLUNTARY

Why are people making so much fuss about the proposed new identity card. It will, after all, be entirely voluntary.

I suspect that the new card will be voluntary if you don't want a driving licence and don't ever want to claim a pension, income support, unemployment benefit or hospital treatment. And as soon as the smarmy, oily politicians have got us carrying little cards they will announce plans to have us all tattooed with our identity numbers instead. I can see them telling us how wonderfully sensible the tattoos will be.

'The tattoos will include national insurance codes and driving licence numbers,' they'll tell us in their sickly, trust-me voices, 'and will be placed in a discrete position on the inside of the forearm. The big advantage of a tattoo is that it won't take up room in your wallet and you don't have to worry about leaving home without it. Citizens will have a choice of three shades of blue ink.'

The government will argue that tattoos will be cheaper and easier to check than identity cards. They will probably get away with all this because although they know that there will, inevitably, be some mild protests from people whom they will dismiss as revolutionaries and anarchists, most citizens will be far too busy watching bloody television to object.

MORE RESPONSIBILITY

My husband has already had one heart attack and has been warned by his doctor to take things easy. However, he has now been offered a promotion at work and says he is going to take it. Do you think this is safe? The new job carries a lot more responsibility and will mean working longer hours.

If your husband elects to take on extra responsibility at work then he will be risking his health and his life for his work. If his work is the most important thing in his life then there is probably little you can do to persuade him to change his mind. But if a more responsible job is simply a means to a bigger pay cheque and a better placed car parking space, then I suggest that you do everything you can to persuade your husband to say 'no' to this added risk. Meanwhile, your husband should listen carefully to his doctor, avoid tobacco and animal fats and, under medical supervision, lose any excess weight and take up a gentle exercise programme.

BLAZING ROW

I had a blazing row with my boyfriend, threw my engagement ring at him and went back to my flat feeling furious. When I got there my flatmate and her boyfriend were watching a blue movie. I sat down with them and had, a few drinks. The movie was about a man and two women and we started off by giggling but soon I realised that my friend had unzipped her boyfriend's trousers and was stroking an enormous erection. To my astonishment she looked at me and said: 'There's enough here for two. Do you want some?' I thought 'Why not?' and joined in. We did everything the people on the video had done and it was the most exciting experience of my life.

A few days later my flatmate's boyfriend brought another movie round. He also brought a friend. I was still feeling angry with my boyfriend—particularly since he hadn't been in touch with me at all. The inevitable result was that the four of us all had sex together.

Now my boyfriend wants us to make up. I don't want him to know what happened but although my flatmate has promised not to say anything she keeps giggling and making oblique references to what went on. I am scared that she will say too much. I would confess but I know that my boyfriend will never forgive me if he finds out what happened. He has a foul temper and is very possessive.

Are you sure you are ready for a long term relationship? And if you are, then are you sure that your current boyfriend is the right person for you to be involved with? If you answer 'yes' to both those questions then maybe you need to think about changing flats or flatmates in order to preserve your secret. If you answer 'no' then your course of action is fairly clear: keep your flatmate and tell your boyfriend that you're not interested in a reconciliation.

....

TOTALLY DEPENDENT

My brother has been in a mental hospital for nine months. I now can't see him ever coming out. He seems totally dependant on the hospital. Mentally he is much better and physically he is as strong as an ox but he seems reluctant to leave. Do you think I could be right?

Patients who have spent a long time in hospital tend to become 'institutionalised' after a while. They are so accustomed to having everything done for them that they become frightened by the prospect of having to cope by themselves. (Incidentally, the staff in such places can also become institutionalised!). The answer is to ask the staff if you can take your brother out on day and weekend trips. Slowly help him regain his confidence so that he can once again cope with the problems of living in the real world.

NOT DOING WELL

Neither of my sons seem to be doing very well at school. They work hard enough and have lots of friends but I'm worried that if they don't do better academically they will have difficulty finding jobs.

Around the world the kids who are top in everything at school invariably end up spending their lives as deputy assistant administrators in the town parks and sewage departments.

PORNOGRAPHIC

I watched a late night film on television the other day. It was quite pornographic. The female characters in the movie were quite unlike any women I've ever met. Don't you agree that it is disgusting that such films should be made? Why don't you start a campaign to have all such films banned.

I'm amazed that you should be surprised and indignant about the fact that some of the characters in a porno movie were unrealistic. Most movies are completely unrealistic. That's why people watch them. The good guy and the bad guy knock hell out of each other for ten times as long as a fight would last in real life. People fly through the air, journey through space, turn into wolves, shrink to the size of ants and travel backwards and forwards through time as easily as real people wander along to the supermarket— and you're worried about the fact that women in porno movies aren't shown spending their days shopping, ironing and picking up the kids from school! I don't approve of censorship of any kind. What the hell is wrong with turning the damned set off if you find yourself watching a programme you don't like?

No LUCK

My husband and I have been trying to start a family for nine months without any luck. Our doctor wants us to keep trying for another few months before he sends us for tests. Can you give us any advice? We are quite desperate to have a baby and have been having sex every morning and every evening.

I think you may be trying too hard. Your husband's body is probably having a job keeping up with the demand for fresh sperm and his ejaculate could well be a bit on the skimpy side spermwise. Try to confine your baby making activities to those days around ovulation when the chances of your being able to turn a hump into a lump are at their greatest. Incidentally, the fact that lots of sex means low sperm counts and decreased fertility suggests to me that maybe the world's overpopulation problem might be solved by encouraging everyone to have more sex.

I LIKE A LOT OF SEX

I like a lot of sex but my husband doesn't seem particularly keen. I'd like to do it every day. He is happy with sex once a week. How can I increase his interest sex? Alternatively, is there anything I can do to reduce my sex drive?

Sex and desire are interlinked and self enhancing. The more sex you have together—and the better it is—the more he will want to make love to you. You can also stimulate his hormones and increase his desire for sex by the careful use of suitable sensory stimulants. Use cosmetics, perfume, sexy lingerie and X rated body language to excite him and you should notice a gradual increase in his yearnings.

....

HOW SAFE ARE CONDOMS?

How safe are condoms? My girlfriend and I had one break on us the other day.

One big survey showed that lovers who used 46,657 condoms had 443 breakages. Of those 443 scary incidents just 19 resulted in pregnancy. (I don't know how many resulted in infection).

To minimise the risk of condom rupture take care when handling them. Remember that most condom tears are started by teeth or finger nails.

....

TRAFFIC WARDEN

I am a traffic warden. I am fed up with motorists being rude to me when I'm just doing my job. Things have got so bad that I no longer dare tell people what I do for a living because they usually make some nasty remark and then never speak to me again. No one seems to like me.

I cannot possibly imagine why you should expect to get any sympathy from me. I am delighted to hear that people are rude to you and that no one likes you. What on earth do you expect? People who take jobs as traffic wardens are, like car park attendants, the sort of people who would have worked as gas chamber attendants during the second world war. Your claim that you are 'just doing your job' is the sort of pathetic, spineless whinge that was heard from regiments of war criminals in the late 1940s. The truth is that you have chosen to perform an entirely unproductive and largely pointless task simply for the money you are paid. No one becomes a traffic warden out of any sense of vocation. You are an overpaid, hired thug and have absolutely no right to complain if you are treated with contempt by everyone you meet. I do hope that makes you feel worse.

BABY ON BOARD

Where can we get a 'Baby on Board' sticker for our car? My wife and I have just had our first child and would like one of these stickers for our car.

Last weekend I drove behind a car which had a 'Baby on Board' sticker attached to and partly obscuring the back window and a rather snotty looking baby in a contraption attached to the back seat. The driver and his companion (presumably the parents who were so keen to advertise their fecundity to following motorists) were both smoking cigarettes. I was mildly amused by this for the chances of their baby being killed or seriously injured by their secondhand cigarette smoke was considerably greater than the chances of their baby being killed or injured by a road traffic accident. This incident confirmed my suspicion that the people who stick these pointless signs on their motor cars are all intellectually deprived.

NEIGHBOURS

We moved into our first house two weeks ago. Taking possession of the key was the proudest moment of my life. Since then life has become a nightmare. The neighbours on one side are very nice but the neighbours on our other side have done everything they can to make life miserable for us. While we were still unpacking they banged on our front door to tell us that the back end of our car was parked in front of their house. There was nowhere else to park because someone else had parked their car in front of our house. I smiled and tried to make light of it but they told me that if I did it again I would receive a solicitor's letter.

Some neighbours are nice and will freely lend you sugar, gardening equipment and sexual partners. Others are just plain nasty. You seem to have unfortunately landed yourself with the breed known as 'neighbouris litigans'. These invariably regard all newcomers as a territorial threat and respond to any modest dispute with the threat of a solicitor's letter. You cannot deflect these people from their single minded pursuit of unhappiness. Ignoring them won't work. They have to be miserable to know that they are alive and you, I'm afraid, are the irritant they need. One possibility is to drive them completely potty so that men in white coats take them away. Alternatively, you can wait until they go out and then paint their front door a different colour and change the number on their house. This will confuse them so much that they may simply spend the rest of their lives wandering the streets looking for their lost home.

NERVOUS

My doctor recently asked me to appear with him on a television programme. I really don't want to have anything to do with it but I got the impression that he expected me to agree automatically. As the date for the filming gets closer I am getting more and more nervous. I really don't want to discuss my personal problems on television. What are my rights?

You have every right not to appear on TV with your doctor—and, just as important, you have every right to expect your doctor to respect your confidentiality and not to discuss you on the programme. Simply tell your doctor how you feel. If he makes any effort to pressurise you into changing your mind then tell him that you will make a formal complaint to the head of the TV station involved. This will probably worry him more than threatening to report him to the General Medical Council.

I am constantly appalled at the number of times patients are used as TV fodder. In my view no doctor should ever appear on TV with his or her own patient. The demands on and expectations of a TV doctor are very different from the responsibilities of a doctor looking after a patient. And in my view filming inside hospitals is voyeurism at its worst.

A SENSIBLE MAN

My husband is a very sensible person. He always keeps an old coat and a pair of rubber gloves in the car in case he has to change a tyre. He always has change in his pocket for car parks and tips. He always knows when the clocks have to go backwards or forwards. He always has a pen that works and if we're going somewhere by car he plans the route down to where we're going to stop for petrol, coffee and toilets. He always wears a pinafore and rubber gloves when he does the washing up and never makes a mess. We go shopping together on Saturday mornings. We make love on Saturday evenings and he always wears a condom even though I have been sterilised. We always make love in the missionary position and although he always comes first he always tries to give me an orgasm by using his fingers (for two years I've had to fake my orgasms simply because our love making is so predictable that I no longer find it exciting). On Sundays we clean the car and do the garden together.

In contrast to my husband I am totally disorganised and without him my life would, I know, be chaotic. I forget things, lose things and once got lost no more than five miles from home.

My husband is faithful and loyal and reliable but he is also dull, boring and predictable. I don't want to hurt him but the thought of spending the rest of my life in the rut he's built for us makes me want to scream. I would like to make love out of doors. I would love to have some adventure in my life.

Are you on probation and is your husband your probation officer? No? Well, stop whingeing then and start taking some responsibility for your own life. It's about time you started making a more positive contribution to the life you lead together. Take your husband by the rubber gloved hand and occasionally lead him astray and into temptation.

For example, here's something you can try now.

Take off all your clothes and put on a coat or dressing gown. Then go and find your husband and, wherever he is and whatever he is doing, unfasten his trousers and kneel down in front of him. When you've got his penis in your mouth shrug off the coat you're wearing so that he can see that you're completely naked. If he's on the course at his golf club don't forget to wave through the players behind or else your husband could be in trouble with the committee.

If that sounds too adventurous for you then at least you'll now realise that you aren't quite the wild, unfettered free spirit you like to think you are!

Encourage your husband to let it all hang out occasionally. Persuade him to wear coloured socks that don't match his tie. Encourage him to accept crinkle cut chips instead of straight edged ones. Talk him into staying in bed one Sunday morning and letting the car stay dirty for a whole week.

And here's a thought: how do you know that your husband isn't sensible and responsible because he thinks you *want* him to be sensible and responsible? Who knows, underneath those rubber gloves and that dainty little pinafore, maybe you could find a wild, tempestous beast of a man just yearning to do unspeakable things to you in the local municipal park.

LOONIES

I recently heard two doctors referring to patients in a mental hospital as 'loonies'. Do men and women in the psychiatric profession often use this sort of language when talking about patients?

Yes, I'm afraid so. Current favourite phrases used by psychiatrists include: Bates Motel (mental hospital); pants waver (nymphomaniac); furniture mover (hysterical patient); and double header (schizophrenic). Incidentally, you may be interested to hear that an official complaint was made to the Press Complaints Commission after I described the majority of psychiatrists as 'dickheads'. The complaint was turned down.

DOCUMENTARY EVIDENCE

Seven years ago I narrowly missed getting a job as a sales executive for a large, national company. Instead I got a job as with a small family firm. The man who got the job I nearly got is now a very successful senior executive with the company. He earns a considerable amount more than I do, has two homes, two cars and a very enviable life style. I have recently discovered documentary evidence which shows that he lied about his qualifications on the application form for the job I so nearly got. What do you think would be the best way to go about making sure that his bosses get this information?

Do you think that if you get him fired you'll get the job you clearly think you ought to have got seven years ago? Or do you just want revenge for the fact that he has been more materially successful than you have? Either way you're allowing your envy to wreck your life. You are carrying around old resentments that are weighing you down, holding you back and souring your spirit. Why do you have to measure your life against his? And why must you keep on looking back when you would get so much more out of life if only you would look forward. There are setbacks and disappointments, narrow misses and 'almost made it' moments in everyone's life. But there are just as many new opportunities and fresh openings if you keep looking to the future. By concentrating on one professional disappointment and by allowing yourself to become embittered by what you clearly see as an injustice you have blinded yourself to fresh prospects.

Why not dump all this old shit? Bury it. Forget it. Burn your tawdry 'documentary evidence' as a symbol of your new determination to start enjoying the present and looking to the future instead of giving yourself (and probably becoming) a pain in the neck by constantly glancing over your shoulder at the past.

....

UNWANTED PROMOTION

I have been offered a promotion at work but I really don't want it. I have seen the way other men of my age ruin their health trying to do jobs in management. I don't have a very demanding job but it suits me fine. I regard my 38 hours of work as 'dead time' but as long as I get paid and can enjoy my family and my hobbies I'm happy. I'm healthy and I don't have much stress in my life. I'd like to keep it that way. My wife is more ambitious and she thinks I should take the promotion, which will mean more money and a bit more status for us both. We've agreed to do whatever you think would be wisest.

If you take on the extra responsibility it is bound to affect your life. No one is going to give you extra money and status without expecting you to work harder and probably for longer hours. You'll have less time and your health will probably suffer. Because you don't really want the extra responsibility you will, I suspect, eventually begin to feel angry and bitter. Your relationship with your wife will probably suffer and may never recover.

On the other hand if you say 'no' to the extra money and status your wife (who is clearly the ambitious one in the family) may feel frustrated.

I feel that you should turn down the promotion and that if your wife still wants more money and status for the family then she should start looking for a career of her own.

You should always try to direct your life in directions which will make you happy. If you don't—if you go down roads which do not lead to happiness—then you and everyone around you will suffer.

··

LARGE, PINK NIPPLES

I am 17 and have very large pink nipples and the inner lips of my genitalia protrude. Are either of these things likely to turn a man off?

Not in the slightest. On the contrary, many men would find these physical attributes extremely attractive.

··

LOCKED IN

Is it true that it is possible for a penis to become locked in a girl's vagina? I have heard that a hospital had to treat a couple who hobbled into the hospital covered only by a blanket and embarrassment.

I've traced the story you heard back to Warsaw, Poland in 1923. The story then was that a young couple had become stuck together while making love in a public garden. They were pulled apart only after a doctor gave the girl an anaesthetic. When the story appeared in the Polish newspapers the couple committed suicide.

Theoretically, it is quite possible for vaginal muscles to go into spasm and imprison a penis. However, such spasms last only minutes and relax spontaneously so I don't think this is a hazard you should worry about too much.

....

SATISFIED AND RELIEVED

I masturbate once a week and it leaves me satisfied and relieved. I have heard that women who masturbate eventually stop having periods and become infertile. Is this true?

I get a lot of letters like this. The answer is 'No'. You will not become infertile, hirsute or even short sighted through masturbation.

....

STRIPTEASE ARTISTE

Neither of us were virgins when we married nine months ago but I have just discovered that my wife used to be a striptease artiste. I am having great difficulty in accepting this. I find it hard to believe that my wife used to take off her clothes so that men could ogle her. And I find it hard to forgive her for not telling me. I confess that I am also haunted by the thought that my wife might also have had sex with men for money. I cannot ask her this outright but I know that it is by no means unheard of for a stripper to augment her income by providing selected patrons with more personal services. I would very much appreciate your advice on how to cope with this difficult problem.

You should try not to allow anything from your wife's past to affect the way you feel about her now. I can think of a thousand occupations more disreputable than taking off your clothes in front of an audience and if you stop to think about it I'm sure that you can too. Try to feel proud of your wife's skills and looks and happy to know that when she strips now you are her only audience. Try to dismiss your other fears from your mind too. Very few strippers sell their bodies for sex and your suspicion is almost certainly unfounded. However, does it matter even if your wife did have sex with men for money in the past? There isn't any real difference between having sex with a man because he's bought you dinner (as many women do) and having sex with a man because he's given you the money to buy your own dinner. Surely the important thing is not what your wife did in the past but what she does now and in the future.

SECRETIVE

My husband is very secretive about what he earns and how much money he has got in the bank. I receive an adequate weekly housekeeping allowance but feel that since we are partners I surely have a right to know more about these things. When my friends talk about their husband's salaries and savings I feel embarrassed because I know far less about my husband than they do about their husbands.

Your husband's secretiveness is certainly odd. I agree with you that you are entitled to know more about financial matters which affect you both. I suggest that you talk to your husband. Ask him how he much he earns and tell him why you feel you should know. There are several possible explanations for your husband's secretiveness. He may, for example, have had a costly divorce in the past.

FLAT ON OUR FACES

My wife wants us to go and live abroad. She says that if we don't go now we'll never go. Part of me wants to go but I have a good job and we have a nice house and I'm worried that if we leave we may fall flat on our faces.

Your wife is right. And so are you. If you don't go now you probably never will. And if you give up your good job and your nice home there is a chance that you will have to crawl back with your tail between your legs within twelve months. But if you don't go you'll never know what would have happened. And getting old and never knowing what might have been is almost certainly worse than getting old and having regrets. This is a decision that you and your wife must make together. I will simply offer you a quote from Augustine of Hippo who once wrote: 'The world is a great book, of which they who never stir from home read only a page.'

•••

MIDDLE AGE

How do you define middle age? I'm 46 and get very offended when people call me middle aged. Surely middle age is 50 onwards?

You're kidding yourself. You are, it is true, on the edge of middle age. But on the wrong edge. If you assume that average life expectancy is 70 years then we're young from 0 to 23, middle aged from 24 to 46 and old from 47 onwards. But what does it matter what you call it? The important thing is that you are as old as you feel (or as someone, probably Groucho Marx, once said, a man is as old as the woman he's feeling). I know 20-year-olds who are 'old' and 80-year-olds who are 'young'. I'm sure that if you stop and think about it you'll know exactly what I mean.

•••

ORAL SEX

My wife loves oral sex. She won't let me have what I call normal sex with her until she has sucked and licked me. Is it normal for a woman to enjoy this sort of thing?

Yes. Believe it or not some women even enjoy sport on television and find drinking alcohol a pleasant experience too. You should regard yourself as a privileged husband for although many women enjoy giving oral sex not all women are equally enthusiastic. Indeed, I have a list of 1,378,259 men whose wives will not perform oral sex on them. Please let me know if you would like any or all of these men to stand in for you and take over your onerous nuptial responsibilities. I can have a queue of 100,000 at your back door by 5.00 pm on Monday.

FRAIL

My husband is in his eighties and very frail. I am thirty years younger. I have no idea whether he has left me anything in his will. I don't even know for sure whether or not he has made a will. Do you think I should mention this? Or do you think I should just accept that he will have made all the necessary arrangements in case anything happens to him?

I think you should explain your fears to him. And be straightforward. I know one man who thought that 'putting his affairs in order' meant writing down a list of all the women he'd had sex with and then putting the women on the list in order of preference.

VULNERABLE

I know that I am very vulnerable to stress and my doctor has warned me that unless I reduce my exposure to stress I may not live long. I have already had one minor heart attack. My problem is that however hard I try I have great difficulty in changing my life in order to exclude stress.

You will never be able to exclude all pressures and stresses from your life; for the very simple reason that you can never control the circumstances under which you live. Whatever you do, and however hard you try to control your life, there will always be people who will bring stress into the world in which you live. Everyone who asks you to make a decision or who hands you responsibility adds to the stress you have to live with. All you can do is learn to control the way you respond to those stresses.

Whenever you feel stress building up, ask yourself what you are worrying about and whether the cause of your anxiety justifies your response. The key is to find the bottom line: decide what is the worst that can happen if your darkest fears are fulfilled. Confront your fears and face the worst; it is the unknown which creates the monsters which will engulf you.

....

A BOTTLE AND A HALF A DAY

My husband drinks too much. He starts drinking in the mornings and just doesn't stop until he goes to bed eighteen hours later. I reckon he gets through a bottle and a half of spirits every day. I have tried to persuade him to seek help but he won't listen to me. He won't even telephone Alcoholics Anonymous, although two of his friends go to meetings and are great believers in AA philosophy. He is sometimes violent and I am worried that he may injure me or one of our children. Our life is miserable. The children are afraid of him and I spend much of my life lying to his boss, providing him with alibis and excuses and cleaning up the messes he makes around the house. I have threatened to leave him but I'm worried that if I'm not there he will just drink even more.

By hanging around and providing your husband with excuses for his drinking you are, I'm afraid, contributing to his problem. You are an accessory. I think you would help him more by walking out, finding somewhere else to live and making it clear to him that you will live with him again only when he acknowledges that he has a problem and seeks help.

....

SPECIAL PARKING

I am delighted to see that some supermarkets now provide special parking places for parents who have children with them. Will you please campaign for more special parking facilities for parents with children?

No, I certainly will not. Why on earth should people who have physical evidence that they have had sex without taking effective contraceptive precautions get special parking privileges? You sound like the sort of idiot who has a 'Baby on Board' sticker on the back of your car. (I never know what I'm supposed to do when I see one of those things but I gather that repeated sounding of the horn is de rigueur since this alarms or wakes the baby, causes it to cry and thereby makes sure that the parents are comforted by the knowledge that their offspring's lungs are in good working order.) The best car parking spaces are already reserved for perfectly fit people who have managed to obtain parking passes either on false pretences or for some absent relative and I can see absolutely no reason why people with children should get parking preference over any other group of individuals. What next? Privileged parking for women with a bra cup size in excess of 38 DD?

....

MONEY FOR A RAINY DAY

I like buying nice things for our home but my husband never seems to want to spend money. I keep telling him that we might as well spend what little we've got because we can't take it with us but he says he wants to keep a few pounds in the bank for a 'rainy day'. I don't see any point at all in putting money on one side for a rainy day that may never come.

The two of you must find a comfortable compromise. Sit down with a piece of paper and a pencil. Write down your total income and then make a list of all your essential outgoings. What is left can be divided into two (not necessarily equal) parts: money for buying 'nice things for the house' and money for a 'rainy day'. Try to think of the 'rainy day' money that your husband wants to put on one side as a sort of security blanket. With a few pounds tucked away safely in the bank you will both be able to wave the appropriate two fingers at demanding or unreasonable employers and others who want to manipulate you or take advantage of you. 'Rainy day' money is sometimes also known as 'fuck you' money. And do think carefully about how much of your income you spend on 'things'. Owning too much 'stuff' can be bad for you, for there is a real chance that you will eventually be owned by your possessions. There are thousands of people around who don't enjoy life because they are constantly worrying about something happening to their car, their collection of porcelain or their wall to wall snow white shag pile carpeting.

UGLY AND UNNECESSARY

I want to have my young son circumcised. I think that foreskins are ugly and unnecessary. Unfortunately, my doctor says that the operation is unnecessary and refuses to arrange for it to be done. My husband says we should follow the doctor's advice.

I am surprised that you should want surgeons to mutilate your son because you consider part of his body to be ugly. Would you expect doctors to cut off your son's ears if you decided that they were ugly too?

The fact is that the foreskin is there for a purpose. It protects the sensitive end of the male organ and can contribute enormously to the pleasure of the owner and his sexual partners.

Circumcision is a barbaric and fairly hazardous procedure. Side effects, including infection and excessive bleeding, occur in 1 in 500 circumcised infants. There is sometimes also damage to the penis itself. In one operation the child's penis was completely destroyed. A sex change operation had to be performed so that the child could be raised as a sterile girl. The girl will require medical monitoring and hormone therapy for the rest of her life.

SWEET SIXTEEN

I'm 17 years old. I'm going out with a girl. She is 16 and I am desperate to make love to her. She's very willing but the only place we can do it is in her parents' living room and they won't leave us alone. Every five minutes one or the other wanders in on some pretext or another and we have to spring apart and pretend to be engrossed in whatever is on the television. It's not as though I'm irresponsible: I've got condoms which I bought just before last Christmas but still haven't used. And it isn't as though I'm going to take her virginity either. I know for a fact that a boy in the fifth form has had her twice.

If you want to enjoy adult pleasures then you must start taking on adult-like responsibilities. Buy a cheap, cardboard suitcase and rent a double room at a nearby hotel. If you can't afford these essentials then get a job delivering newspapers or cleaning cars and save up your pennies until you can. And while you're saving up you'd probably better save up for some new condoms too. The antiques that have made their mark on the inside of your wallet are probably fit only for the National Condom Museum in Pontefract.

....

BURGLED

My home has been burgled three times in the last four months. What can you suggest?

Put up a large notice saying: 'This building is patrolled by free roaming, unmuzzled, rabid guard dogs at night and occupied by highly strung, easily offended weight lifters during the day. The building is used for the development of bioactive viruses for military purposes, for the storage of highly toxic acids and for experimental techniques designed to neutralise nuclear waste. You are currently being photographed and bombarded with marker rays. In accordance with Ministry of Defence regulation DF/tr/957 we must inform you that the marker ray system we use may induce cancerous growths. Please try to leave the area quietly to avoid setting off the noise-triggered sprinkler system which has been filled with a solution designed to neutralise escaping toxic acid fumes. We are advised that this solution dissolves human skin and causes blindness within 12 hours. Close the door when you leave to prevent the escape of dangerous fumes. Please visit a specialist hospital immediately for decontamination and 28 days' observation. For their safety please tell doctors treating you to use full protective clothing in accordance with Ministry Regulation TRW/8376y. Warn them that you are contaminated with Beta Heptazone Dichlorylate and possibly infected with the virus Instabilicus Oriflamivitis. For further information qualified medical personnel only may telephone the Ministry's Hazardous Substances Research Department.'

....

RENT OR BUY?

I want to buy a small house but my husband says he's happier to rent. He says that if we buy somewhere then we'll be stuck with it if we want to move. He also says that if we buy we'll have to do all the maintenance and so on whereas if we rent all that will be someone else's problem. I want to buy somewhere so that we can have a place we can really call our own. My husband says I've just got an overdeveloped nesting instinct.

You don't have to buy a place of your own in order to have somewhere you can call home. 'Home' is a concept based more on mental attitudes than on the legal ownership of bricks and mortar. There are significant hazards associated with property ownership. Thousands of people have discovered that owning a home can mean being a prisoner. Those who bought their homes when prices were higher cannot sell and move unless they can afford to take a huge financial loss. The constant stress and strain of buying, owning and maintaining a property is so great that people who rent their homes live on average 5.2 years longer than people who buy the property in which they live.

. . . .

TERRIBLE NAG

My wife is a terrible nag. I can never do anything right. If I sit down with the newspaper for five minutes she calls me lazy. If I've been working on the car or in the garden I have to strip down to my underpants—and leave my dirty clothes outside—before she'll let me into the house. If I want to have sex I have to give her 24 hours' notice—and I'm only allowed to have it twice a month. I hand over all my earnings (including those from a part time job I have) and have to provide her with an account of how I spend the £5 a week pocket money I receive. My life is really miserable.

Beg, buy or borror a French maid's outfit, a blue movie and six cans of beer. Go outside and roll around on your vegetable patch for five minutes. When you're satisfied that you can't get any dirtier lie under the car and change the oil. Then walk briskly into the house—studiously ignoring your wife's bleatings. Put the blue movie into the video recorder, open yourself a can of beer and sit down in her favourite armchair. She will by now be hysterical. Hand her the French maid's outfit and order her to put it on and to then go into the kitchen and cook you a large plateful of egg and chips. She will either do as you tell her (in which case you can regard her as successfully 'broken in') or she will leave you and go back to live with her mother. Either way you win.

. . . .

NOISY SEX

Is it acceptable for a woman to make a noise during sex? When my boyfriend makes love to me I frequently feel like shouting out but I try to keep quiet because it somehow doesn't seem ladylike to make a noise. Do you think he would mind if I let myself go a little more?

I doubt very much if he would mind. An entirely unreliable recent survey of retired civil servants showed that

83.7% of them preferred noisy sexual partners. Favourite phrases included: 'Do it to me!', 'Yes, yes, big boy!' and 'Oh, my God, I'm coming, I'm coming!'. Many men like their partners to use words which would not be considered appropriate for use in the drawing room. And it is not at all uncommon for some very refined women to use earthy four letter words at moments of high passion. Please don't feel shy or embarrassed about showing your feelings in the bedroom. The average man's dream woman has been described as someone who can be a cook in the kitchen, a housekeeper around the home and a whore in the bedroom.

HAVING THE BOSS FOR DINNER

Last weekend my husband brought his boss home with him for dinner. I knew he was coming and had really made an effort and prepared a lovely meal. I spent a whole week's housekeeping budget on the food and wine. After the meal I sat on the sofa next to my husband's boss and while we were talking he casually put his arm around me and started stroking my shoulder and slipping his fingers inside my blouse. I didn't like to say anything because I know that he has a lot of power over my husband's career but as soon as I could I went out into the kitchen to fetch more coffee. While I was there my husband came in and told me that he had a headache and was going to bed. He asked me to stay up to entertain his boss! I was very surprised. My husband doesn't normally get headaches and even if he had had a stinker I would have thought he would have soldiered on in order to try and make a good impression on his boss. 'You've made a real hit with him,' whispered my husband. 'He really fancies you so be nice to him!' At that point I suddenly realised what was going on. I asked my husband if he expected me to have sex with his boss. I was absolutely flabbergasted when he told me that it was up to me but that it would do his career a lot of good if I did. I didn't know what to do and so when my husband went back upstairs I was in quite a daze when I went back into the living room with two cups of coffee.

The coffee never got drunk. My husband's boss had my clothes off in less than five minutes and he had sex with me twice. After he had gone home I stayed downstairs alone and couldn't believe what had happened. I felt really ashamed of myself and very dirty. But I have to admit that I found the sex very exciting. When he started taking my clothes off I didn't give him any encouragement but I quickly got excited and it showed. I never usually have orgasms when my husband makes love to me but I didn't have any trouble having orgasms with his boss. When my husband eventually crept downstairs to see how things had gone I screamed abuse at him. That was over a week ago. I now feel very confused. I have told my husband that if he ever tries to put me in a position like that again I will leave him. But I can't forget what happened and I have an awful feeling that if a similar situation occurred again I would not put up any resistance. I almost feel like a whore.

You are a whore. And your husband is a pimp. Having successfully managed the deed why be afraid of the words? Since your aim in making love to your husband's boss was at least partly to improve or secure your husband's wage packet you were screwing for money: that makes you a whore. A potentially high class hooker, but a hooker nevertheless.

I have deliberately been blunt because I think that you have to face reality if you are to decide how best to deal with what has happened and what seems certain to happen again.

Did you really 'allow' your husband's boss to have sex with you because you were in a daze? I think that is a rather weak claim. I suspect that the first reaction of most women would have been to try to brain their husband with a kitchen implement. Are you really so weak and insipid that you simply lay down and opened your legs? Would you unquestioningly do anything for your husband rather than disappoint him? Or did you go to bed with this man because you realised that a promotion for your husband would mean a bigger wage packet? Or did you, perhaps, agree to what

happened because you were excited by the prospect of
having sex with a virtual stranger? Did the knowledge that
your husband was upstairs make the whole incident even
more exciting?

And what about your husband? Was he liberal with your
favours simply to further his own career? Or was he turned
on by the knowledge of what was happening? Is he going to
want to watch next time?

Only when you are both honest with yourselves about
what has already happened will you be able to decide how
best to deal with the next time. And one way or another I
am pretty sure that there will be a next time.

Finally, I have a question for you. Did your husband get
promoted? Or did his boss screw you both?

....

THE KINDEST WAY

What is the kindest way of telling an otherwise scrupu-
lously clean friend that he smells like a dirty ash tray? I
don't want to hurt his feelings.

You have to pick the method to suit the individual. Mrs
Ann-Marie Confucius, whose philosopher husband was
a keen smoker of French cigarettes, told me that she
tricked her partner into giving up his noxious habit by
persuading him to ask himself the question 'Why are we all
here?' every time he thought about lighting up. On the
other hand, the inimitable Sophia Machiavelli, widow of the
much loved Niccolo, told me that she cured her political
activist husband of smoking by persuading his numerous
friends to drop oblique hints. And Mrs Dolores
Torquemada, whose husband helped mastermind the
cruellest aspects of the Spanish Inquisition, held lighted
matches under her husband's testicles until he agreed to
substitute peppermints for cigarettes. You could simply try
telling him that you love kissing him but that you find the
taste of stale tobacco a real turn off.

....

READ WITH INTEREST

I would like to thank you for your campaigns about drug safety.

I believe that for every medical horror story which gets into print a hundred are suppressed by fears or threats of litigation, a thousand disappear into history because no one finds out about them and ten thousand never even surface because everyone involved keeps their mouths shut and so no one (including the patient, if he or she is still alive, and his relatives and friends if he or she is not) hears about what has happened.

Thousands of big, fat, rich drug company bosses run the world as if they own it and those members of the medical profession who are not incompetent or blind to what is going on are usually too frightened to say anything lest they ruin their careers. (Those who stay silent lest they damage their careers are right to worry: whistle blowing is professional suicide in the healing professions. I am advised that I am the subject of more complaints—usually coming from other doctors or drug companies—than any other qualified doctor in the country.)

....

THE PHYSICAL SIDE OF MARRIAGE

My husband died 5 years ago, after twenty very happy years of marriage. When a nice young couple moved in next door last year I was able to help the wife by looking after her two young children while she went shopping and so on. In return her husband Barry would help me out with odd jobs. My video broke the other day and having seen Barry going to his shed in the garden I followed him. When I opened the shed door I was extremely embarrassed to discover him masturbating over a men's magazine. I shut the door and rushed away. A few minutes later Barry knocked on my door. He explained that his wife had told him that she could no longer bear him touching her. She had, he said, told her to get his sex somewhere else.

As he explained things I felt very sorry for him. When he asked me how I coped with being alone I was honest with him. I told him that I did find it difficult. The physical side of marriage was always very important to me. It came as a complete surprise when he put his arms around me and asked me if he could kiss me. We ended up in bed together. Since that occasion he calls round regularly. His wife either doesn't care or doesn't suspect. I have no illusions. I know he wouldn't leave his family and I wouldn't want him to. But I do enjoy the physical relationship we have. From talking to his wife I believe that Barry has been telling me the truth about their relationship. Do you think it's all right for us to carry on or should I stop having sex with him?

I love that phrase 'the physical side of marriage'. When I hear it I always get a vision of a happily married couple digging the garden together or sweating it out on a matched pair of exercise bicycles.

Whatever she may have told him (or you) there is a risk that your neighbour will hit the roof when she finds out where her husband has been parking his travelling organ. And there's also a risk that one or both of you will fall in love—thereby putting a sizeable cat among the pigeons. You have to weigh up the risks and decide whether the potential downside is worth the upside. I assume, by the way, that you are taking precautions to avoid pregnancy and infection.

••

LONELY HEARTS

After my husband left me I answered a lonely hearts advertisement and met a great bloke. It was lovely being half of a couple again. He was much more adventurous than any of my other lovers and when he asked if he could take erotic photos of me and video us making love I agreed. He said I could keep all the pictures at my place but since I have two young children I said I would rather he kept them. Two weeks ago he brought a contact magazine round and said he wanted us to meet other couples for sex. I was shocked and said 'no' at first. However, eventually I was so worried about losing him that I agreed. I went along to another couple's home with him and then chickened out and just sat and watched. My boyfriend was furious with me afterwards. He now says that if I don't agree to group sex with strangers he will show the photos and video to everyone I know.

Grit your teeth, steel yourself and call his bluff. Tell him that you're going to report him to the police for attempted blackmail. Try to prepare yourself to cope with the worst that he can do. This man is a slimy bastard with the soul of a lawyer and the morals of a politician. He could crawl under a carpet without wrinkling it. If you give in to him now there is no knowing where or when his demands will end.

....

TERRIBLE LUCK

My best friend is always moaning about the fact that she has terrible luck with men but I think she's at least partly to blame for the trouble she gets into. She always seems attracted to men who treat her badly—ones who drink too much, gamble, go out with other women or knock her about. When I pointed this out to her she agreed but explained that the nice, sensitive men she meets are always dull and boring. The really funny thing is that she always tries to reform the bad men she collects into the good guys she could have had in the first place but thought too boring!

I'm afraid that you will not be able to change your friend. And I certainly don't think you should even hint that you might hold her partly to blame for the problems she finds herself in. As a friend you should restrict yourself to offering advice, succour, support, comfort and a boxful of paper tissues whenever things get bad.

MISTAKE

I've been married for nine months and I'm beginning to think that I might have made a terrible mistake. I run my own hairdressing and beauty business which I've built up from scratch and I'm keen to expand. I also play quite an active role on the Management Committee at a local health club. Two weeks ago I was flattered to be invited to become a governor of the school which our two daughters attend. My husband, who has a job with the local authority, is not very supportive. He is opposed to me expanding my business and can't understand why I'm not content to just stay at home, cook his meals and iron his shirts. I find it difficult to understand why he is happy with an undemanding routine job and a social life that seems to revolve around the television set.

There are two sorts of people in this world: the players and the spectators. The players do things, take chances and put their careers, lives and wealth on the line. The spectators criticise and offer their opinions but prefer to stand on the sidelines because they are frightened to take risks. It sounds to me as though you are a natural player and your husband is a committed spectator. It is unlikely that anything will change your respective roles in life (though it is true that some players occasionally tire and become spectators and some spectators succumb to temptation and become players for a while). If you can both understand this—and accept and become accustomed to your different roles in life—then your marriage may thrive, blossom and survive in a way that eludes other, apparently better matched pairings.

POLITE AND RESPECTFUL

Why are young people so rude? I am 72 years old and when I was a child we were all taught to be polite and to be respectful to our elders. Young people these days don't seem to have any manners at all.

Fashions change and many traditional, old fashioned courtesies are pushed aside by progress but generally speaking people remain much the same: some are polite, thoughtful and kind hearted while others are rude, aggressive and selfish. The percentage in each category is as great among pensioners as it is among pubescents. It's a myth that old people are all patient, sensitive and well mannered. Stand in any queue anywhere and you're as likely to get your shins bruised by orthopaedic shoes and carelessly brandished Zimmer frames as you are by Doc Martens.

....

DRESSED LIKE A WOMAN

When a neighbour of mine dressed up as a woman and walked along the street outside our home he was arrested by the police. What offence was he committing? I am a woman and I often wear slacks or trousers. I am slightly alarmed by the thought that I might be arrested for wearing the wrong sort of clothes.

There are no laws forbidding the wearing of clothes originally designed for members of the opposite sex. But the existence of laws has little relevance to whether or not you are likely to get arrested. And the laws which do exist are often interpreted in bizarre ways. What logic is there in a legal system which results in the arrests of men and women who try to disrupt the hunting of perfectly innocent wild animals while allowing politicians to walk around our streets unhindered?

....

FLYING

I worry about flying. Can you give me some advice, please?

No. If God had intended us to fly he would have made aeroplane seats big enough to sit in.

INJURED

Our next door neighbour, who is divorced and in his 50s, was recently injured in a car accident. I started popping in to help. Some days he is in so much pain that he cannot move about and has to stay in bed all day. One day, after he had been in bed for three days, I asked him if he wanted a bed bath. I was amazed when I saw how well endowed he was. He developed an enormous erection very quickly and climaxed as soon as I touched him in that area. He was very embarrassed and apologised profusely. He explained that he really missed the physical side of marriage. I told him I didn't mind at all and admitted that I was flattered. When I left he gave me a £20 note. I told my husband and he laughed, saying it was the easiest £20 I'd ever earn. Since then I have given my neighbour a bed bath twice a week—with similar results. On each occasion he gives me a £20 note. The last but one time I saw him he asked if he could touch my breasts. I didn't see any harm in it since he didn't want me to undress or anything. And the last time he asked me if I would use my mouth to bring him off. I told him that I would have to think about that. I haven't told my husband about these latest developments nor, indeed, about my regular income from the 'special' bed baths, and I realise that the way we are heading it won't be long before I am having full sex with him. He is a very nice man and far better endowed than my husband. I'm pretty sure my husband wouldn't mind— he and I have had sex no more than half a dozen times in the last three years and our relationship is more businesslike than loving—and the money is certainly very useful, but I am confused. I have never slept with another man but I am really tempted. If I stop things developing any further I know I will regret it but I suspect that if I let things carry on the way they are heading I will be letting myself in for problems I will not be able to deal with.

Life is full of problems. An out of control lorry could career through your living room. A lump of ice could fall from an aeroplane and crash through your roof. You could be falsely arrested or told by your doctor that you have an incurable wasting disease. You could be bitten by a rabid dog, kidnapped by Welsh terrorists or invited to be a Tory party candidate at the next Euro elections.

We get one go each at life. It doesn't sound as though you're having a lot of fun with your go. I think you probably deserve a few more orgasms before you get shut up in an old people's home. A team of highly trained specialists who I invited to comment on your problem suggested that you take all the usual precautions and bonk yourself senseless. They weren't specialists in human relations, they were car mechanics, but their advice merits serious thought.

....

REDUNDANT

When my husband was made redundant the only job he could find was 250 miles away. We couldn't sell our house so he got digs with a widow close to his new job. He comes home on Friday evenings and goes back very early on Mondays. At first things weren't as bad as I'd feared. We both appreciated one another more and instead of just sitting around the house at the weekend we made an effort to do things together. The enforced absences did wonders for our sex life too. Then, six weeks ago a young couple made an offer for our house. I was excited but when I rang my husband he made all sorts of excuses for keeping things as they are. In the end we had a big row and I slammed down the telephone in tears. I couldn't sleep and so the next day I caught a train and went to see him. To my horror I discovered that the widow my husband lodges with is five years younger than I am—and very good looking. I found out that my husband and this woman live together as husband and wife during the week. When I confronted him with what I had found out my husband said that he loves us both and wants to carry on with things as they are. He is adamant that he will not give up this woman.

Have you thought about telling your husband that you will accept his terms on condition that he allows you to make similar arrangements of your own? Maybe the thought of you spending Mondays to Thursdays playing trains and tunnels with a toy boy from the local weights and measures department might make him realise what he is asking you to accept?

....

NO TIME

I am a nurse working in a busy hospital. Because of your columns and books a lot of patients now demand that we explain things to them. Would you please tell your readers that we don't have time to explain things. People should just trust us to do what is best for them.

What a stupid, callous and uncaring person you are. Where did you do your nursing training? Conservative Party Headquarters? No one with more than half a brain would trust doctors and nurses to do what is best for them. Mistakes made by doctors and nurses are now a major cause of ill health and death. I was tempted to ask you how you would feel if you were in hospital and no one told you what they were doing to your body—or why they were doing it. But I doubt if you have the imagination to understand the question. So, in order to protect patients in the area where you live, I have arranged for the hospital where you work to keep you on permanent bed pan duty. Hopefully, you will soon get fed up with your malodorous duties and seek work elsewhere. Might I suggest that you look for something exceptionally hazardous? Maybe you'd like to open a kosher restaurant in Beirut...

....

A SOURCE OF FRUSTRATION

I have a very responsible job but at the office where I work all the real power lies with the administrators—who do not

have any responsibility at all! I have to make many decisions every day and if things go wrong I am held
accountable but I do not have the authority I need. I find
this a tremendous source of frustration and would appreciate your comments.

Much of the stress in the world has been created
because responsbility and authority have been separated. When I worked as a general practitioner during the
early part of the Boer War I was constantly in trouble with
the bureaucrats because they had the authority I needed in
order to fulfil my responsibilities to my patients. Before I
eventually resigned to become a lot of trouble for a living, I
found that I could exert some degree of control over the
bureaucrats by threatening to force them to accept some of
my responsibility whether they wanted it or not. So, for
example, I found that the men-in-cheap-suits-with-pens-in-
their-breast-pockets became remarkably compliant if I told
them that unless they did what I considered to be best for
my patient I would, if the patient died, list them as a
contributory cause of death on the death certificate. This
had an almost magical effect—producing instant action
from even the most lethargic of administrators. I suggest
that you try to find your own way to 'persuade' the accursed
administrators to trade a little of their authority for some
of your responsibility.

··

THE CONDOM FELL OFF

I have been going out with a boy for five months. We have
sex a lot. He has got a small penis. This doesn't bother me
as I love him. But can a boy with a small penis make me
pregnant? We haven't used any contraceptives. We tried
a condom but it was much too much big for him and just
fell off. I am too nervous to go to the doctor for advice.

The size of your partner's penis is of no significance as far
as conception is concerned. A bullet from a palm sized

automatic can kill just as effectively as a bullet from a machine gun. I suggest that you visit a local family planning clinic. You may find the prospect of doing so embarrassing but, believe me, you'll be far more embarrassed when you have to book in at the maternity clinic.

··

A DIFFERENT PILL

For years I have been taking a pill for my blood pressure. Last week a new doctor gave me a different pill. When I went back to complain he told me that although the pill looked different it contained the same ingredients. Can he be right?

Yes. Drug companies make two sorts of pills: brand name drugs (which are expensively advertised) and generics (which are chemically identical to the branded versions). It's all very much like supermarkets selling 'own brand' beans and well known branded beans. I suggested that doctors should prescribe generic rather than brand name drugs in my first book—*The Medicine Men*—which was published back in 1975. Everyone laughed. Now many doctors, pharmacists and politicians agree with me that if doctors prescribed generic drugs instead of expensively advertised brand name versions, hospitals (and patients) would save billions of pounds. There's a bonus: since there would be fewer drugs around and less confusion, mix ups would happen less often and patients would be safer.

··

BECOMING A NUN

My daughter wants to become a nun. How can I dissuade her?

Why do you want to dissuade her? Nuns have a pretty good life. Other people do all their worrying for them. They don't have to concern themselves with dreary everyday problems and they get to travel everywhere first class.

IN A HURRY

I was collecting a prescription from our local surgery when my doctor rushed out in a terrible hurry. I asked the receptionist what the emergency was. She told me that the doctor was late for a lunch being given by a big drug company. When I expressed surprise she told me that my doctor had lunch at the expense of a drug company two or three times every week. This doesn't seem right to me. I'd always thought of doctors as being above bribery but what other reason can drug companies have for buying meals for doctors?

Being a doctor used to mean being part of a profession. No more. Doctors are now just another arm of drug company marketing departments. Clearly, doctors would not need to be bought free meals in order to be persuaded to prescribe important, life saving new drugs. Doctors are given free meals by drug companies trying to flog drugs which may have little or no advantage over existing products. The smaller the advantage the drug offers the harder the drug company has to try in order to get doctors to prescribe it. You may feel that this means that really crappy drugs are promoted with tremendous enthusiasm and very expensive meals.

BEING HONEST

While we were in bed my boyfriend asked me if his whatsit was as big as all the other whatsits I'd had. I always believe in being honest so I told him it wasn't. In fact I told him that it was the smallest I'd ever seen. When he asked me if I preferred big ones I said I did. He said that it wasn't the size but what you did with it that really counted but I said that was nonsense. He then went all quiet and disappeared. Half an hour later I found him in the bathroom crying.

I'm surprised he hadn't slit his wrists. How would you feel if he had told you that your breasts were too small and that you had a harbour big enough for the QE II to be moored? Men worry about these things and like women to be tactful. In this instance tact usually involves a certain amount of dishonesty. If you love him would it have really hurt you to lie a little?

....

BAD BACK

I would like to see an osteopath about my bad back but I am frightened to do so lest I upset my doctor who has been trying hard to heal me for months. The osteopath I would like to visit has an excellent local reputation.

Most of the doctors I know who have had back trouble have visited osteopaths for help. Why not tell your doctor what you're planning? The chances are high that he will approve wholeheartedly. Incidentally, the number of people now visiting alternative health care practitioners is so great that osteopathy, acupuncture and so on are just as much a part of mainstream medicine as are men and women in white coats with stethoscopes round their necks.

....

RUDE REMARKS

We are a group of traffic wardens who were very offended by your recent rude remarks about our profession. We demand an apology.

Piss off. It was a traffic warden who wouldn't turn a blind eye when a woman left her car parked outside the vet's so that she could take her injured cat in for treatment ('can't make any exceptions'). It was a traffic warden who slapped a ticket on a car while the driver helped his pregnant wife into hospital ('only doing my job'). It was a traffic warden who stuck a ticket on a car from which a disabled woman was struggling to extricate herself ('more than my job's worth not to'). I am delighted to have received thousands of offensive, aggressive and semi literate letters from traffic wardens. It makes my heart warm to know that I have reached out and touched so many objectionable bastards in one go.

To those who have threatened revenge on the streets I would like to point out that I drive a very old, very large blue Bentley which is far too heavy to tow away and which has wheels which are too large to clamp. You can recognise my Bentley easily because in the place where the Queen's car flies a royal standard my car flies a skull and crossbones. Most traffic wardens are so stupid that when they see the flag they salute rather than give me a ticket and I have every confidence that despite this revelation this state of affairs will persist.

• •

DESPERATELY FRUSTRATED

My wife's best friend recently came to stay with us. She and her husband broke up about nine months ago. Two days ago while we were in bed my wife asked me if I'd like to make love to her friend. She told me that her friend is feeling desperately frustrated but although she wants sex she doesn't want to start a new relationship. My wife said that her friend found me quite sexy and had told her that she wished she had someone like me to go to bed with. I was absolutely shocked by my wife's suggestion. At first I thought my wife was just joking but it eventually became quite clear that she was very serious. Her friend is a little plump but very attractive and making love to her would be very nice. But do you think I should?

What on earth are you asking me for? Your wife's friend is keen to play trains and tunnels with you. Your wife is quite happy about this planned adventure. And instead of getting down to business and making a lonely woman very happy you're wasting time writing to me? My guess is that you must be a civil servant working in some sort of planning department. You have spent so much of your life avoiding responsibility that you are now incapable of making any decisions at all. Actually, I don't think there is much hope for you. Any man who can describe the prospect of fully authorised adultery as 'very nice' has about as much style and soul as a knitted toilet roll holder. Just for the record I seem to remember that D.H. Lawrence, the expert on mining and body part nomenclature, once argued that a natural sexual relationship should involve three, not two, individuals.

....

BREACH OF CONFIDENTIALITY

My mother has been ill for several months. She asked me to go with her when last she went to see the doctor. Before we went I asked her what she wanted to tell the doctor and what she wanted to know from him. I then wrote down a list of questions to ask and a list of symptoms that seemed important. When we got into the surgery the doctor asked me who I was and then refused to let me stay. He said it would be a breach of patient confidentiality for me to stay in the room. Reluctantly I left but before I went I handed him the list I'd made. He laughed when he saw it and said something about 'another nutter'. Was the doctor right to refuse to allow me to stay with my mother?

You did exactly what you should have done. Sensitive, thoughtful doctors who care about their patients heartily approve of patients making lists of questions—and taking notes. Your mother's doctor sounds as though he probably obtained postgraduate qualifications in compassion and sensitivity at the Mengele Memorial Social Engineering Department at the downtown University of Barnstaple. I suggest that your mother find an alternative practitioner. Indeed, she would probably be better off visiting a local vet.

HAPPILY MARRIED MAN

I am a happily married man. Last weekend I attended my sister's fiancé's stag night. During the evening her fiancé, who is German and looks so pleased with himself that we refer to photos of him as 'smug shots', got quite drunk and made a pass at me. He told me that he found me very attractive and wanted to go to bed with me. When I told him that I was strictly heterosexual he confessed that he is bisexual. He then made it pretty clear that he would not regard having homosexual relationships as being unfaithful to his wife. I was—and am—appalled. What should I do? Should I warn my sister about the man she has now married?

What a pity you didn't say something before she married him. Your sister could then have cancelled her wedding and done something better with the day—like shampooing the carpets or painting her toe nails.

I normally recommend a 'blind eye—closed mouth' policy to individuals who ask whether they should share their knowledge of an individual's sexual indiscretions with the individual's partner. But in this instance I will make an exception. I think you should tell your sister now what sort of man she has married. I cannot think of a word that accurately describes your sister's fiancé — but the word 'Conservative' perhaps most accurately conveys my feelings of contempt and revulsion.

SEX SIX TIMES A MONTH

My husband and I are both in very good health and 80 years old. We enjoy sex at least six times a month. Do you think we will damage our health?

No. Regular sex will help keep you both fit, active, supple, healthy, alert and smiling. People who don't get enough sex become irritable, wheezy, mentally stodgy and defaced with wrinkles and liver spots. It was people who don't get enough sex who voted Conservative at the last election.

AND FINALLY...

'I've had 120 Christmas cards this year!' she said, proudly. 'Isn't it wonderful to have so many friends?'

I looked around. The mantelpiece, the top of the TV set, the sideboard and the windowsills were packed with colourful greetings cards.

It was an impressive sight.

But what she said made me think about the way we devalue one of the most important assets in our lives: friendship.

She didn't have 120 *friends*. Most of those cards were from casual acquaintances.

And I wondered if she had ever really thought about the true nature—and importance—of friendship.

❂ ❂ ❂

The world you and I live in has become a cold, cruel, heartless place.

The people we pay to look after us when the fates are against us, to take care of us when we most need support and help and to protect us from cruelty and injustice—the justly accursed politicians, lawyers, doctors and clergy— have, by and large, abandoned and betrayed us.

Most politicians don't give a damn about the people they are paid to represent. They are inspired only by self interest, lust and greed.

The law has become a discredited, distrusted sick joke. Policemen and lawyers constantly abuse their authority. Their primary instinct is not to protect us but to abuse, arrest and imprison us.

On the whole doctors now do more harm than good. The medical establishment has been bought by the drug industry and today's men and women in white coats are an insult to the memory of Hippocrates and Paracelsus and are little more than a twice paid marketing arm of the international pharmaceutical industry.

The clergy have completely lost touch with reality and have become an irrelevance.

Administrators—the faceless, nameless, characterless grey men in suits who now run the world—absorb authority like a sponge and reject responsibility.

The bottom line is that you should no longer expect your country to look after you—or to provide you with education, justice or healthcare.

You and I are on our own.

Except for our friends.

❂ ❂ ❂

Author, friend and newsletter writer Chevalier Harry D. Schultz, whom I much respect and whose investment newsletter is the best way I know of to keep up with what is going on in the world, told me recently that he regarded good friends as more important than anything—even health. Harry is listed in the *Guinness Book of Records* as the world's highest paid investment adviser.

My message for you this year is that you should take great care of your friends. They are the most valuable asset you have.

Choose your friends with care and then treasure them.

Your loyalty to true friends should take precedence over everything else in your life.

Remember: there is a world of difference between friends and acquaintances.

The former you can ring at 3 in the morning for advice and help and support.

The latter will simply add to your annual Christmas card collection.

To win a new friend you must first *be* a friend.

And you must work at that friendship. You must invest time and energy and caring.

If you end up with half a dozen true friends then you will be truly blessed.

True friendship is an asset which will never tarnish and never devalue. And no one will ever be able to take it away from you.

Vernon Coleman
January 1995

Published by the European Medical Journal

The Traditional Home Doctor

Vernon Coleman

Packed with practical health tips

Contents include:

- ANOREXIA - 7 tell-tale symptoms
- ARTHRITIS - 9 ways you can help yourself
- ASTHMA - 6 tips to help you cope
- BABY NOTES - 25 things to know about a newborn baby
- BACKACHE - 7 ways to avoid and 8 ways to conquer it
- CANCER - 10 ways to help fight cancer and win
- CHOKING - life-saving techniques
- COLDS AND FLU - 7 tips to help you stay healthy and 5 tips to help you fight colds and flu
- COT DEATH - 6 tips to keep your baby safe
- CRAMP - a simple remedy that works
- CRYING IN BABIES - 8 causes and the solutions
- DRY SKIN - 5 tips for making it feel soft again
- EMERGENCIES AND ACCIDENTS - practical advice
- FOOD - eating healthily
- HEADACHE - 3 ways of dealing with headaches
- HEART DISEASE - 8 tips to protect your heart
- HIGH BLOOD PRESSURE - 9 ways to keep it down
- HOME NURSING - 10 tips to help patient and nurse
- HYSTERECTOMY - 5 facts women should know
- INDIGESTION - 7 tips for sufferers
- IRRITABLE BOWEL SYNDROME - 4 solutions
- OVERWEIGHT - 18 tips to help you slim successfully
- PROSTATE GLAND - facts all men should know
- RELAXATION - how to relax your body and your mind
- SLEEPLESSNESS - 17 tips
- SNORING - 5 tips to help you stop it
- STRESS - 11 tips to help you conquer the stress in your life
- •• and much, much more! ••

ISBN 0 9521492 7 3   232pp   £9.95

Available from Book Sales, European Medical Journal, PO Box 30, Barnstaple, Devon EX32 9YU. Please write for a catalogue.

Published by the European Medical Journal

Food for Thought

Your guide to healthy eating

Vernon Coleman

Packed with easy-to-use, up to date, practical information,
Food for Thought is designed to help you differentiate between
fact and fantasy when planning your diet.
The book's 28 chapters include:

- Food the fuel: basic information about carbohydrates,
  protein, fat, vitamins and minerals
- When water isn't safe to drink—and what to do about it
- How what you eat affects your health
- Why snacking is good for you
- The mini-meal diet and the painless way to lose weight
- Quick tips for losing weight
- The Thirty-Nine Steps to Slenderness
- 20 magic superfoods that can improve your health
- The harm food additives can do
- 20-point plan for avoiding food poisoning
- Drugs and hormones in food
- Food irradiation, genetically altered food, microwaves
- 30 common diseases—and their relationship to what you eat
- How to eat a healthy diet
- 21 reasons for being a vegetarian
- How much should you weigh?
- How to deal with children who are overweight

ISBN 0 9521492 6 5
192pp   paperback   £9.95

Published by the European Medical Journal

How to Conquer Pain

A new and positive approach to the problem of persistent and recurrent pain

Vernon Coleman

A fully revised and updated edition of *Natural Pain Control.* This book tells you

- Factors which influence the amount of pain you feel
- Doctors, drugs and pain control
- How to get the best out of pills
- Alternative therapies that work
- The unique Pain Control Progamme
- How to use your imagination to conquer your pain
- How to sleep when pain is the problem
- The magic of the TENS machine
- Learn how to relax and control your stress
- How to measure your pain
- •• and lots, lots more! ••

What they said about the first edition:

☞ A clear and helpful handbook for pain sufferers… Perhaps most important of all is the way in which it brings pain down to a manageable level and gives self help ideas for sufferers.
The Guardian
☞ Full of good ideas *Mother and Baby*
☞ A new and positive approach *Keep Fit*
☞ An authoritative guide to this universal problem
Bournemouth Evening Echo

ISBN 0 9521492 9 X 192pp paperback £9.95

Available from Book Sales, European Medical Journal, PO Box 30, Barnstaple, Devon EX32 9YU. Please write for a catalogue.

Published by the European Medical Journal

Bodypower

The secret of self-healing

Vernon Coleman

A new edition of a book that hit the Sunday Times and Bookseller 'Top Ten' charts.

- How your body can heal itself
- How your personality affects your health
- How to use bodypower to stay healthy
- How to stay slim for life
- How to conquer 90% of all illnesses without a doctor
- How to improve your eyesight
- How to fight cancer
- How to use bodypower to help you break bad habits
- How to relax your body and your mind
- How to use bodypower to improve your shape
- •• and much, much more! ••

What they said about the first edition:

☞ Don't miss it! Dr Coleman's theories could change your life
Sunday Mirror

☞ If you've got Bodypower, you may never need visit your doctor again, or take another pill! *Slimmer*

☞ A marvellously succint and simple account of how the body can heal itself without resort to drugs *Spectator*

☞ Could make stress a thing of the past *Woman's World*

☞ Shows you how to listen to your body *Woman's Own*

☞ Could help save the NHS from slow strangulation
The Scotsman

ISBN 0 9521492 8 1 160pp paperback £9.95

Available from Book Sales, European Medical Journal, PO Box 30, Barnstaple, Devon EX32 9YU. Please write for a catalogue.

Published by the European Medical Journal

Mindpower

How to use your mind to heal your body

Vernon Coleman

A new edition of this bestselling manual

- A new approach to health care
- How your mind influences your body
- How to control destructive emotions
- How to deal with guilt
- How to harness positive emotions
- How daydreaming can relax your mind
- How to use your personal strengths
- How to conquer your weaknesses
- How to teach yourself mental self defence
- Specific advice to help you enjoy good health
- •• and much, much more! ••

What they said about the first edition:

☞ Dr Coleman explains the importance of a patient's mental attitude in controlling and treating illness, and suggests some easy-to-learn techniques *Woman's World*
☞ An insight into the most powerful healing agent in the world—the power of the mind *Birmingham Post*
☞ Based on an inspiring message of hope *Western Morning News*
☞ It will be another bestseller *Nursing Times*

ISBN 1 898947 00 7
256pp paperback £9.95

Available from Book Sales, European Medical Journal, PO Box 30, Barnstaple, Devon EX32 9YU. Please write for a catalogue.

Published by the European Medical Journal

Why Animal Experiments Must Stop

And how you can help stop them

Vernon Coleman

"The most damning indictment of vivisection ever published"

"Essential reading for anyone wishing to counter the arguments of the vivisectors"

Dr Coleman analyses all the pro-vivisection arguments one by one—and destroys them.
The moral, ethical, scientific and medical arguments are all dealt with.

Animal tests can produce dangerously misleading information. Penicillin kills cats and guinea pigs. Aspirin kills cats. Digitalis is so toxic to animals that it would never have been cleared for humans, but it remains our most useful heart drug. Yet practolol, which was judged safe after animal tests, caused damage to human patients and had to be withdrawn.

Dr Coleman makes it clear that animal experiments are useless today and have always been useless.

This book also describes the alternatives to animal experiments. It offers readers a 10-point plan to help them make sure that vivisection is stopped, putting an end to one of the world's most barbaric practices.

ISBN 0 9521492 1 4

128pp   paperback   £6.95

Available from Book Sales, European Medical Journal, PO Box 30, Barnstaple, Devon EX32 9YU. Please write for a catalogue.

Published by the European Medical Journal

Betrayal of Trust

Vernon Coleman

Betrayal of Trust follows in the tradition of Vernon Coleman's most iconoclastic and ground-breaking books—*The Medicine Men, Paper Doctors,* and *The Health Scandal.*

Dr Coleman catalogues the incompetence and dishonesty of the medical profession and the pharmaceutical industry and explains the historical background to the problems which exist today. He shows how drugs are put onto the market without being properly tested, and provides hard evidence for his astonishing assertion that doctors now do more harm than good.

To support his claim that drug companies use animal tests to get their drugs on the market, Dr Coleman lists scores of widely prescribed drugs which are reguarly prescribed for patients, despite the fact that there is evidence showing that the drugs cause serious problems when given to animals.

Drug companies are, he explains, in a 'no lose' situation. If a new drug seems safe when given to animals, the company making it uses that evidence to help get the drug a licence. But if a new drug causes problems when given to animals, that evidence is ignored as irrelevant! Only patients lose.

"When animal experiments are stopped," says Dr Coleman, "they will never be reintroduced. The moral, ethical, scientific and medical evidence all supports the contention than animal experiments must be stopped now."

ISBN 0 9521492 3 0
160pp paperback £6.95

Available from Book Sales, European Medical Journal, PO Box 30, Barnstaple, Devon EX32 9YU. Please write for a catalogue.

Published by the European Medical Journal

Relief from IBS

Simple steps for long-term control

Vernon Coleman

- Causes and symptoms of Irritable Bowel Syndrome
- The two-step control programme
- How you should change your diet
- How to look after your digestive system
- Relief from wind
- Watch out for foods that make your symptoms worse
- Stand up for yourself
- Build up your self-confidence
- Learn to relax your body and mind
- How worrying more can help you worry less
- Tips to help you cope with stress
- Take control of your life

1 898947 03 1
96pp   paperback   £9.95

Available from Book Sales, European Medical Journal, PO Box 30, Barnstaple, Devon EX32 9YU. Please write for a catalogue.

Published in hardback by Chilton Designs

Toxic Stress and the Twentieth-Century Blues

Vernon Coleman

Never have I read a book that is so startlingly true. I was dumb-founded by your wisdom. I have long been a fan of your writings. You will go down in history as one of the truly great health reformers of our time.

(Extracted from a letter to the author)

We live in a world which would seem, on the surface, to offer us all the material things we need. Few of us go cold and hungry and the miracles of science and technology surround us – offering us opportunities that our ancestors would have found unbelievable. But underneath this veneer of contentment, society is sicker than ever. Violence and crime against property are increasing; the incidence of mental illness is rising reapidly, the divorce rate is higher than ever with more than 1 in 3 marriages failing. Examine society closely and you will find that sadness, frustration, boredom and fear are rife – and how many of us can honestly claim never to have felt one, if not all, of these emotions on a regular basis?

In this important book, Vernon Coleman examines the underlying causes of the sadness in our society and, most importantly, offers a programme of help and guidance to those who are suffering from 'the twentieth-century blues'. This thought-provoking book reveals many harsh and frightening aspects to the world we live in, but will also help sufferers regain their zest for living by overcoming loneliness, conquering stress and finding new purpose and meaning in life.

0 9503527 4 8
107pp £10.95 hardback
Available from Chilton Designs Publishers, PO Box 47, Barnstaple, Devon EX32 8YT

FICTION BY VERNON COLEMAN

The Bilbury Chronicles

The first in a series of novels following the adventures and exploits of a young GP who begins work in an idyllic Exmoor village

0 9503527 5 6 230pp £12.95 hardback

Bilbury Grange

The second novel in the series which sees the newly married doctor moving into his new home – a vast, rambling country manor in desperate need of renovation

0 9503527 7 2 247pp £12.95 hardback

The Bilbury Revels

The third novel in the series sees the village of Bilbury united in a fundraising effort after a devastating storm hist the village

1 0898146 05 5 270pp £12.95 hardback

Bilbury Pie

A collection of short stories featuring the characters from the Bilbury series of novels

0 8980146 15 2 149pp £9.95 hardback

The Village Cricket Tour

The story of an amateur cricket team on tour in the West Country

0 9503527 3 X 173pp £9.95 hardback

The Man Who Inherited a Golf Course

The hero of the story wakes up one morning to find that he has inherited a golf course in his uncle's will

0 9503527 9 9 237pp £12.95 hardback

Thomas Winsden's Cricketing Almanack

A spoof of the cricketing 'bible', Wisden

1 898146 00 4 128pp £9.95 hardback

Mrs Caldicott's Cabbage War

A charming story telling of one woman's fight against society and her battle to keep her independence after the death of her husband. A truly inspiring book

0 9503527 8 0   150pp   £9.95 hardback

Deadline

A thriller set in London and Paris and featuring ex-investigative journalist Mark Watson

1 898146 10 1   164pp   £9.95 hardback

Available from Chilton Designs Publishers, PO Box 47, Barnstaple, Devon EX32 8YT